FORTUNATE SON

The Church in the Wildwood
Dr. William S. Pitts
Public Doman

High Flight
John Gillespie Magee, Jr
Public Domain

Baby Boy Francis
Copyright © 2013
Doc Schneider
Used by permission

Front & back cover photos © Brooks Eason
Used by permission

Fortunate Son: The Story of Baby Boy Francis
Copyright © 2019
Brooks Eason

ISBN: 978-1-948679-69-5
Library of Congress Control Number:2019947927

Cover design by David Warren.

Published by WordCrafts Press
Cody, Wyoming 82414
www.wordcrafts.net

FORTUNATE SON

The Story of Baby Boy Francis

To Carol,

Best wishes,

Brooks

BROOKS EASON

WordCrafts Press

For my families

the methodist home hospital

REV. L. D. HAUGHTON
SUPERINTENDENT

818   WASHINGTON   AVENUE
NEW ORLEANS 13, LOUISIANA
TELEPHONE TWinbrook 5-7709

May 2, 1957

Mr. and Mrs. Paul Burrow Eason
1505 Rogers Drive
Tupelo, Mississippi

Dear Mr. and Mrs. Eason:

We are happy to inform you that your home has been approved
by the Methodist Home Hospital for the placement of a child. You
understand, of course, that placement will be made only when and if
a suitable child becomes available for you. At that time we shall
notify you.

Your cooperation and assistance during the study of your home is
appreciated.

Sincerely yours,

(Mrs.) Elsie W. Wessel, please note change y
Social Work Supervisor   name)

Rev. L. D. Haughton
Superintendent

EWW:nw
cc: Mrs. Gay
    Mr. Stokes
    Miss Parish
    Mrs. Carpenter

the methodist 🅗 home hospital

REV. L. D. HAUGHTON
SUPERINTENDENT

615   WASHINGTON   AVENUE
NEW ORLEANS 13, LOUISIANA
TELEPHONE TWinbrook 3-7709

August 8, 1957

Mr. and Mrs. Paul B. Eason
1505 Rogers Drive
Tupelo, Mississippi

Dear Mr. and Mrs. Eason:

We received your letter concerning your application for a second
child. We know that you do get anxious at times about the long waiting
period. However, there is just nothing we can do about it. We try to
find the best possible home which we have for a baby when the baby is
ready to go. When we have the baby which fits best into your home,
you will be notified through your Welfare Department. We cannot tell
you when that will be. We do know that waiting can be tiresome, but
we do believe your waiting is rewarded in the end. We are so glad that
you are happy with your little girl.

Sincerely yours,

(Mrs.) Elsie W. Wessel
Social Work Supervisor

EWW:nw

A METHODIST INSTITUTION OF MERCY

the methodist home hospital

618   WASHINGTON   AVENUE
NEW ORLEANS 13, LOUISIANA
TELEPHONE   TWinbrook 5-7709

REV. L. D. HAUGHTON
SUPERINTENDENT

April 15, 1958

Mr. and Mrs. Paul Burrow Eason
1505 Rogers Drive
Tupelo, Mississippi

Dear Mr. and Mrs. Eason:

This is your notice that you may file your petition to adopt
Paul Brooks Eason who was placed in your home by The Methodist Home-
Hospital on September 19, 1957 for the purpose of adoption.

Enclosed you will find the revised birth certificate for Paul Brooks
Eason. We are asking that you check this certificate carefully for
errors before signing it. We would then like for one of you to sign
the certificate using jet-black ink and return it to The Methodist Home-
Hospital.

Mr. Max M. Schaumburger, 621 Whitney Building, New Orleans, will be
happy to handle your adoption for you. He will, upon your instructions
directly to him, prepare the necessary legal documents and forward
them to you for your signature. After that, when the case is fixed,
you will be advised of the date to appear in this city for the court
hearing.

It has been a pleasure to work with you and we appreciate the
cooperation which you have given during this time.

Sincerely yours,

(Mrs.) Elsie W. Wessel
Social Work Supervisor

Rev. L. D. Haughton
Superintendent

EWW:mw
Enc.
cc: Mrs. Gay   A METHODIST INSTITUTION OF MERCY
     Mr. Stokes, Miss Parish, Mrs. Carpenter, and Mr. Schaumburger

Prologue

A last will and testament has no legal effect until the death of the person who signed it, and its provisions often remain a secret until the loved ones gather round after the funeral for the reading. Only then do they learn who will get what.

Wills and their consequences, which involve not only death and money but also love, control, grief, and greed, play a central role in many famous works of fiction. How those contemplating death choose to dispose of their assets discloses a great deal about them, and the attitudes and actions of those they leave behind are even more revealing. Disputes over inheritances bring out the worst in families. Blood relatives become sworn enemies and commit four of the seven deadly sins—pride, greed, envy, and wrath. Fights over what would appear to an outsider to be mere trinkets damage relationships beyond repair.

Jarndyce and Jarndyce, an interminable dispute over a large inheritance, serves as the backdrop for the intricate plot of *Bleak House,* regarded by many as Dickens' finest novel if not his most famous. The case in chancery court drags on for generations and comes to a merciful end only when legal costs exhaust the entire estate and the matter is abandoned for lack of anything to fight over. Dickens described the lengthy proceeding in a single sentence: "The little plaintiff or defendant, who was promised a new rocking-horse when *Jarndyce and Jarndyce* should be settled, has grown up, possessed himself of a real horse, and trotted away into the other world."

The book I have written is a memoir, not a novel. The story also spans generations and also involves a dispute over a large inheritance, though the dispute itself was brief and no enemies were made.

Two wills, one executed by a rich man and the other by his granddaughter, are central to the story. The first, signed in 1962, contained a clause that was likely an afterthought, was never intended to take effect, and never did. And yet, more than four decades later, the clause almost made me a wealthy man, a result the man who signed the will never could have foreseen. Indeed, he may have gone to his grave in 1969 without even knowing I existed. Nor did his granddaughter intend to make me an heir. To the contrary, she sought to disinherit me. But, as fate would have it, she nearly achieved the opposite. Her will, which she signed in 1978, led not only to my being found more than a quarter of a century later but also to the possibility that I would inherit a fortune from her grandfather.

Ultimately, however, the fortune I got was not in the form of material wealth. Instead it was this: Without the two wills signed by the man and his granddaughter, I never would have learned the true story you're about to read.

Chapter 1

It was a Tuesday morning in June 2004. The day had started like any other. I walked the dogs, ate breakfast while reading the paper, then drove downtown to work. I was in my office on the 14th floor of the Trustmark Bank Building when my phone rang. It was my father, Paul Eason. He rarely called me at work but had just listened to an intriguing voicemail. He was calling to tell me about it.

Daddy was 82 and lived by himself in Tupelo, Mississippi, in the home where I grew up. It was the only home he and my mother Margaret ever owned. She had died five years earlier in the bedroom they shared for more than 40 years. I lived three hours south of Tupelo in Jackson, where I had practiced law for two decades.

The message was from a woman in New Orleans, also a lawyer. She said her firm was conducting a nationwide, court-ordered search for Paul Eason, age 46. I go by my middle name, but my first name is Paul and I was about to turn 47. I told Daddy I would return the call.

Why a court in New Orleans would order someone to search the entire country for me was a mystery. A theory occurred to me, but after all these years it didn't seem possible. Because I didn't know the reason for the call, I decided not to identify myself as the Paul Eason the lawyer was trying to find. I would just say I was Brooks Eason and was returning the call she had placed to my father. But when she came to the phone, she already knew who I was.

"I can't believe we found you."

"What is this about?"

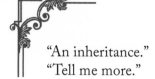

"An inheritance."

"Tell me more."

That was the day I began to learn the story that had been a mystery to me all my life, the story of my birth and second family. In the days that followed, I found out that my name was Scott Francis—or rather that it had been—for the first year of my life. I was nearly 50 years old, but until then I didn't know I had started life with a different name, much less what it was. My name, as well as the rest of the story, had been a secret. This is the story of how I learned the secret. But this story is about more than that. It is also about the wonderful life my parents gave me, about my exceptional daughter and granddaughter, who was born just days after Daddy received the voicemail, and about how times and attitudes changed from when I was born until she was born.

Chapter 2

One of my first memories seems clear to me even now. I'm in my small bedroom on the back corner of our house on Rogers Drive in Tupelo. There is a pine tree outside one window, a sweet-gum outside the other, and the closet door is covered with marks recording my sister's height and mine as we grew up. In the closet is my toy chest, which will make its way to my own home 25 years later after Mama paints Ann Lowrey's name on it along with balloons and a teddy bear. It was in this room that I hid my transistor radio under the covers and listened as the St. Louis Cardinals won back-to-back National League pennants in the late 1960s.

I've tried to summon an unpleasant memory from my childhood bedroom, but I can't seem to do it. I'm sure there were some, but it's been more than 40 years since I packed my bags and left for college. The closest I can come is in the summer of 1963, when Mama and Daddy gave me a complete baseball uniform, cap down to cleats, for my sixth birthday.

A few days later, when my neighborhood friends showed up with ball, bat, and gloves to play in the vacant lot beside our house, I ran inside to put on my new uniform so I could show it off. My buddies weren't wearing uniforms, but that didn't stop me. I got dressed and stood before the mirror in my room admiring myself and adjusting my new cap to just the right angle. Then I went back outside. My friends had gotten tired of waiting, changed their minds, and left.

My earliest memory of my bedroom is from three or four years earlier, also in the summer but at night. I'm lying on the bottom bunk, the top bunk three feet above me. The small space is comforting, not confining. It's my cocoon. The windows are open, screens keeping the mosquitoes at bay. Mama is lying beside me, reading to me. Through the open windows come the songs of katydids, tree frogs, and nighthawks along with the sweetness of honeysuckle, which mixes with the smell of Mama's cigarettes. I hear a train in the distance. The tracks are a mile away, but the sound carries in the night.

But do I really remember Mama and the reading and the train? Or only being told about them? Or do I just remember remembering? Trying to pin down our earliest memories is a tricky business. Do we actually recall events from our earliest years? Or do we build our first memories from bits and pieces of many memories? From family stories and photos? How much is folklore?

I have claimed for more than 50 years that I caught 27 fish the very first time I went fishing, and that I used raw bacon for bait. Going through old photos, my wife Carrie found one of me sitting beside the creek east of our home on Rogers Drive. I'm wearing a cap, holding a cane pole, and staring down at the water. The date on the photo showing when it was developed is May 1959. I was not yet two years old. How could I remember that I caught 27 fish? How could I have even counted to 27? Maybe Mama kept track and told me later. Before I could fish by myself, she would have been the one baiting my hook, unhooking the tiny fish I caught, and throwing them back. Even if the number is right, it would be more accurate to say I caught fish 27 times than to say I caught 27 fish. The creek was four feet wide and I fished in the same spot. I must have caught the same fish over and over.

My first memory of Daddy is among my very favorite memories of all. He had already been the Scoutmaster of Boy Scout Troop 12 for 10 years when I was born and he took the troop camping every month. When I was little, I would watch him pack his gear and leave on Friday afternoon. When he returned a day or two later, I would greet him at the kitchen door and he would pick me up and hug me, then turn me around and tickle the back of my neck with his chin whiskers. He would tell me about the troop's

6

adventures and I would inhale the smell of the smoke from the campfire he'd sat beside the night before. I couldn't wait until I was old enough to go with him. I'm now in my seventh decade, but I still love camping and campfires, and the wonderful smell of wood smoke still reminds me of him.

I can't say which of these memories is my first, but it doesn't matter. All are wonderful memories from a happy childhood. I grew up in a good place at a good time. My life was stable and secure. My parents were devoted to each other and to my sister Margie and me. But they didn't hover; there were no helicopter parents back then. My friends and I had freedom to roam, to explore the woods during the day and play kick the can in the neighborhood at night. During the summer we would listen at sunset for the mosquito truck—the fog machine—then run behind it in the dense white cloud of DDT, oblivious to the risk. We caught lightning bugs and put them in jars with holes punched in the top, took them to the darkest place we could find and watched them light up the night, then let them go. We played every game imaginable in the vacant lot next to our house, many that we invented. When Daddy got home from work, I would get our gloves and baseball and he and I would play catch. The creek where I caught my first fish was next to the vacant lot. My friends called it Eason's Creek, which made me proud, and we explored every inch of it, swimming in the deep pools and catching crawdads, tadpoles, fish, and turtles and, on rare occasions, a snake.

Our neighborhood was filled with children. The Cagles, Carrolls, and Trammels all lived within a hundred yards of our house, as did the boy with the best nickname, Horsefly Duncan. But my best friends in my class, Jimmy Ingram, Dan Purnell, and Nat Langston, all lived in Sharon Hills, a neighborhood nearly a mile from ours. The main road there made a circle. If you lived on the outside, your address was Sharon Hills; on the inside, it was Lynn Circle. I never knew why; maybe the developer had two daughters. On summer mornings I would go to Sharon Hills, or one or more of my friends would come to Rogers Drive. We played outside all day, coming in at noon just long enough for a glass of milk and a peanut butter and jelly sandwich on white bread. By mid-summer we were as brown as a berry.

To get from Rogers Drive to Sharon Hills, I had to walk or ride my bike past Legion Lake, then up the driveway and through the big backyard of a house between the two neighborhoods. My buddies had to do the reverse to get from Sharon Hills to Rogers Drive. Jack and Frances Reed, two of Tupelo's leading citizens, lived in the house with their two sons and two daughters. Jack later ran for governor, Jack Jr. coached my fourth grade flag football team, and Scott was my doubles partner on the Tupelo High School tennis team. The Reeds never objected to our constant trespassing and never would have dreamed of doing so. If they had, I would not have been able to spend my summer days with Dan, Nat, and Jimmy. More than 50 years later I still remember their birthdays and phone numbers.

Carrie's childhood was not at all like mine. In her first 14 years she moved all over America, from Texas to New York, then to Oregon and Illinois. She lived in nine cities in eight states altogether. From the time I outgrew my crib until I left for college, I slept in the same bed in the same room in the same house. Over and over Carrie had to leave her school and her friends and start a new school and make new friends. I went to the same schools with the same friends from kindergarten through high school, and Jimmy was my first college roommate. Carrie's parents divorced when she was 12. Mine were four months away from their 50th anniversary when Mama died in September 1999. Her funeral was at the First United Methodist Church in Tupelo, where her father had been the preacher more than six decades earlier, Daddy's parents were members, she and Daddy got married, and Margie and I were baptized. Daddy later served on the administrative board and Mama sang in the choir. When Daddy died in 2013, his funeral was held there as well.

Daddy was the finest man I've ever known. Many sons say that of their fathers, but many sons of other fathers have said that of mine. He always did the right thing. Daddy was a Boy Scout leader for 60 years, from before he married Mama until after she died. He helped raise three generations of boys in Tupelo, serving as leader and role model for more than a thousand Scouts. On his 90th birthday Congress honored him for his lifetime of service with a resolution that was read aloud on the floor of the House of Representatives in Washington. Daddy got the honors, but it was Mama who took me fishing during the day and read and sang to me at night, who painted beautiful pictures, and who kept my sister and me while Daddy went camping. And it was Mama who could wiggle her ears.

There is much talk these days about privilege. I had the most valuable privilege of all: family privilege. Our house was small, I didn't get my first car until I was 21, and I didn't fly for the first time until my first wife and I left for our honeymoon. We were not rich in money but, in what really matters, I was the richest boy in town.

Chapter 3

1886 was an eventful year in America. Coca-Cola was invented in Atlanta and Geronimo surrendered in Arizona. The Statue of Liberty was dedicated and Grover Cleveland became the first and only president to get married in the White House. He was 49, his bride, Frances Folsom, 21. Most Americans didn't seem to mind the age difference. Two years later Cleveland won the popular vote but lost in the Electoral College to Benjamin Harrison. Four years after that he won both. By winning the rematch with Harrison in 1892, Cleveland became the first and only president to serve two non-consecutive terms.

Also in 1886 a group of Methodist churches in Louisiana and Mississippi established a maternity home called Methodist Home Hospital. A facility that would accommodate 40 unwed mothers was ultimately built in New Orleans on the corner of Washington Avenue and Annunciation Street four blocks north of the Mississippi River. In addition to caring for pregnant girls and women, the home had a nursery for their infants and served as an adoption agency.

A dedicated staff of social workers ensured that the babies would go to good homes. Women from all faiths and all over the country were welcome without regard to ability to pay. Most of the doctors on the staff contributed their services. A brochure from the 1950s described the home as "An Institution of Mercy Supported by the Methodist Church That They Might Have Life."

A number of famous Americans, notably Ty Cobb and Al Jolson, were born in 1886. Three of my ancestors were also born that year and a fourth got married. I knew only one of the four, but without two of them I would not exist and without the other two my life would not be the same. The three births occurred nearly a thousand miles apart and were spread over eight months. Ethel Jane Land, Mama's mother, was born in January on a farm outside Garlandsville, Mississippi. In August Minnie Henby was born in Platteville, Wisconsin. Sidney Hugh Davis was born less than a month later in Morristown, New York. My ancestor who got married that year was Henry Felgar Brooks, called Harry by all who knew him. He married Rose Cochran at her family's home in Greensburg, Pennsylvania, in February.

Ethel was later called Grandma by her many grandchildren, of whom I am the youngest. She was the third of 10 children—eight girls and two boys—born to the former Mary Elizabeth Williamson and Henry Clay Land, who was named for the Great Compromiser and perennial presidential candidate from Kentucky. Shortly after the turn of the century, when Ethel was a teenager, the Land family moved from Mississippi to a farm near Carlton, Texas, southwest of Fort Worth. They made the trip by train, their livestock in the cattle car behind them. Ethel later attended business school in Tyler, then took a job working for a judge in Fort Worth. There she met and was courted by Harry Brooks, who by then was Dr. Brooks, a Methodist minister. They married in February 1910.

Harry was older than his bride. He led Ethel to believe he was 10 years older, but the difference was actually much more than that. Harry had another secret as well—a daughter from his previous marriage to Rose Cochran whose existence he decided to keep to himself. He concealed both the marriage and the daughter for nearly 30 years until the day when a middle-aged woman knocked on the door of the parsonage where he and Ethel lived with their children. When asked why she was there, she announced that she was looking for her father. The truth about Harry's daughter was thus revealed, but he was able to take the secret about his age with him to the grave. He kept other secrets as well.

It's hard for me to picture Grandma as a young woman. She was 71 and had snow-white hair by the time I was born and had

11

already been a widow 15 years. But she lived another 20, most of them in Tupelo, where she crocheted placemats, baked homemade bread, and beat me at checkers. At night she put her false teeth in a coffee cup beside her bed. Whenever someone had the bad manners to ask her age, she would say she was as old as her tongue but a little bit older than her teeth. That's true of all of us—we're born with tongues but no teeth—but in her case the difference in age was more than for most of us. The difference in age between Grandma and her spouse was more than for most of us as well.

Like Ethel and her family, Sidney Davis also moved west, in his case from New York to Wisconsin, then south to Missouri. And like Harry and Ethel, he and Minnie Henby got married in 1910. Their wedding was in St. Louis. As was the custom at the time, both couples began having children right away. The first born in the two families were both girls and both named Elizabeth. Elizabeth Brooks was born in 1911, Julia Elizabeth Davis the following year. The Davises decided to call their daughter Betty. They could not have named her for actress Bette Davis, who was only four years old when their own Betty was born.

Over the course of the next decade both families continued to grow. Elizabeth Brooks was followed by a brother and three sisters, the last two born minutes apart in March 1921. Mama was not the youngest member of the Brooks family only because she came into the world just before her identical twin, Marjory. The twins probably came as a surprise to Harry and Ethel. A century ago couples rarely knew either the gender or the number of the babies they were having. Minnie Davis also gave birth three more times after her first child, but she had no twins. After Betty came three boys, first Roger, then Sidney. William, the youngest, was born in September 1921, six months after Mama and Marjory.

My paternal grandparents, Margaret and Cliff Eason, whom we called Momie and Daddy Cliff, had 10 grandchildren. Momie was pronounced like Mommy but spelled differently, maybe because she wasn't our mother but maybe because that's the way her children spelled it. Nobody alive today knows the reason. Daddy Cliff and Momie were born two months apart in northwest Mississippi in

1898. They got married in January 1921 and started a family even faster than the Brookses and Davises did. Daddy was a honeymoon baby, born nine months and two weeks after the wedding. They named him Paul for Daddy Cliff's older brother Paul Mims Eason, who had been killed three years earlier fighting the Germans in World War I in the Meuse-Argonne Offensive in France.

October 8, 1918, the day Sergeant Alvin York of Tennessee became a hero by single-handedly killing more than 20 German soldiers and capturing 130 more, was also the day Paul Mims Eason died. The war ended only five weeks later. It may seem tragic to die so near the end of a war, but even more tragic were the fatalities on the very last day of World War I, when thousands of soldiers were killed even after the parties agreed to end the fighting. The armistice was signed before dawn, but the ceasefire did not go into effect until the 11th hour of the 11th day of the 11th month, and the commanders did not call a halt until then. More men were killed and wounded during those few hours on the morning of November 11, 1918, than on D-Day a quarter of a century later. Private Henry Gunther from Baltimore, the last man killed in World War I, died at 10:59 a.m. His military record includes this sad sentence: "Almost as he fell, the gunfire died away and an appalling silence prevailed."

Daddy Cliff turned 20 before the war ended, but he couldn't fight in it. He was rejected by the Army because of an injury with a pencil lead that required plastic surgery to rebuild his left eyelid. Plastic surgery then was not what it is today, and the eye always gave him trouble.

Momie and Daddy Cliff did not give Daddy his Uncle Paul's middle name but instead chose Burrow, which was Momie's maiden name. Thirty-six years later Mama and Daddy followed their lead and chose Mama's maiden name for my middle name. In the years after Daddy was born, Momie and Daddy Cliff had three daughters: Myra, whom the family called Tut (which rhymes with put, not but); Annie Maude, whom everyone called Puddie; and Doris, the baby, who was 10 years younger than Daddy. Daddy also had a family nickname. He was Bubba to his sisters, their husbands, and children but to nobody else. Doris didn't get a nickname, at least not one that I ever heard, perhaps because her siblings were old enough by the time she was born to pronounce her real name.

Sidney and Minnie Davis continued west as their family grew, moving first to Baxter Springs, Kansas, then to Tulsa, where they lived the rest of their lives. Sidney, whose nickname was Misty for reasons that no one recalls, was a mining engineer by education. After graduating from the University of Wisconsin, he took a job surveying land to identify potential mining prospects, often in the wilderness of the West and often on horseback. His employer wanted to pay him a straight salary, but Sidney arranged to take part of his compensation in fractional interests in the mines developed from the prospects he recommended. He was good at his job and began to accumulate valuable holdings when he was still quite young.

While the Davises were living in Baxter Springs, Sidney's name appeared in a short article in the *Joplin Globe*, the newspaper in the larger town just across the Missouri state line. The story was about a fishing trip he and other mine operators were taking to Lake Taneycomo, a reservoir on the White River in southwest Missouri created when the Powersite Dam was completed in 1913. The headline declared that "Fish Had Better Take To The Woods."

On the same page of the *Globe* I noticed an appalling want ad. At the top of the ad was a drawing of a man on horseback wearing full Klan regalia, on the bottom a post office box for sending applications. In the middle were these words: "100 PER CENT AMERICANS ARE WANTED, None Others Need Apply, Knights of the Ku Klux Klan." The Klan's popularity in America peaked in the 1920s with membership estimated at four million. The date of the newspaper was March 13, 1921. Three days later, nearly 500 miles southwest of Joplin in Amarillo, Texas, Mama and Marjory became the last two children born to Harry and Ethel Brooks.

The Davises soon moved from Baxter Springs to Tulsa, where Sidney continued his career as a successful entrepreneur and

businessman. Before his 40th birthday he founded the Ozark
Chemical Company, which produced sulfuric, hydrochloric, and
phosphoric acid for use in the oil and gas industry. The company was
successful but not entirely because of Sidney. Events in Colorado
that began when he was still in his teens were crucial to its growth.

In 1901 a young dentist named Frederick McKay opened his
practice in Colorado Springs and discovered a disturbing phenomenon: The teeth of many of the city's residents, especially children,
were the color of chocolate candy. He also found that the brown
teeth were surprisingly resistant to decay. The cause of the condition,
which was known as Colorado Brown Stain, remained a mystery
for three more decades. The phenomenon was not restricted to
Colorado. Residents of Oakley, Idaho, were afflicted after a new
water source was tapped. In Bauxite, Arkansas, a company town
owned by the Aluminum Company of America, known as ALCOA,
brown teeth were also prevalent. In a community only five miles
away the residents' teeth were white but had many more cavities.

H. V. Churchill, the chief chemist at ALCOA, was concerned
that the brown teeth in Bauxite would be blamed on aluminum
and set out to find the cause of the problem. Tests conducted in
1931 showed a high level of fluoride in the town's water supply.
Until then the existence of naturally occurring fluoride in water was
unknown. Subsequent tests of the Colorado Springs water supply
showed high levels of fluoride as well. The finding was followed by
extensive research to determine if there was a safe level of fluoride
that would reduce decay in teeth but not turn them brown. The
results were positive and Grand Rapids, Michigan, became the first
city in the world to fluoridate its water supply in 1945.

The following year Ozark Chemical Company merged with
another company Sidney had co-founded, Mahoning Mining
Company, which mined fluorspar in southern Illinois and western
Kentucky. The new company was called Ozark Mahoning Company, and Sidney served as the chairman of its board of directors.
In addition to its mining and chemical operations, the company
had an oil and gas exploration business as well as a sodium sulfate
division with headquarters in Texas.

The company began using fluorspar to make fluorine specialty chemicals in the early '50s. Not long after that, Crest became the world's first fluoridated toothpaste. Sales of the new toothpaste grew exponentially thanks to an ad campaign featuring portraits of smiling children holding up reports from their dentists and declaring "Look, Mom—no cavities." Norman Rockwell painted the portraits using children in his hometown of Stockbridge, Massachusetts, as models. Sidney's company took advantage of the new opportunity and began making fluoride compounds and selling them to toothpaste manufacturers. At one point the company owned and operated the only facility in the Western Hemisphere that converted fluorspar into fluoride for toothpaste. Under Sidney's leadership the company became large and profitable and he amassed a significant fortune.

In the mid-1930s the Davises' oldest child and only daughter, Betty, married a young lawyer named Tom Francis. He contracted polio on their honeymoon and the marriage didn't last. Before splitting up, however, the couple had one child, a beautiful, bright-eyed daughter born in November 1938. They named her Julia for her mother and called her Julie.

By the mid-1920s Harry and Ethel Brooks and their five children had moved from west to east, from Texas to Mississippi. For Ethel it was a return to her home state, but for all the others it was their first time in Mississippi. In the years that followed, Harry served as the pastor of a series of churches in Jackson and north Mississippi, with the family moving from one parsonage to the next. The Brooks children left schools and friends behind almost as often as Carrie did 40 years later.

By 1934 Elizabeth had married a wealthy plantation owner from the Mississippi Delta, and the rest of the family had moved to Tupelo, where Harry served as the minister of the First Methodist Church, a beautiful Gothic Revival church on Main Street built in the late 1800s. The church later became the First United Methodist Church when the Methodist Church and the Evangelical United Brethren Church merged in 1968 to form a single denomination. Among the loyal members of the congregation in Tupelo when

Harry became the preacher were Momie, Daddy Cliff, and their four children.

Daddy Cliff was a banker through and through. He worked in banks from the time he graduated from high school in 1916 until he retired in 1973, the year he turned 75. He and Momie were living in Byhalia, a small town just south of Memphis, when Daddy was born. They soon moved across the state to Belmont, where they lived for several years, then settled in Tupelo in 1926. Four years later Daddy Cliff started a successful career that spanned more than four decades at Peoples Bank & Trust Company, which is now called Renasant Bank. The bank survived the Depression and Daddy Cliff rose through the ranks to become its president despite never having attended a day of college. College was a luxury a hundred years ago. Intelligence and a strong work ethic, both of which Daddy Cliff possessed in abundance, were more important than a degree.

The bank's main office was on Main Street, two blocks east of the Methodist Church. Even after he became the bank's chief executive, Daddy Cliff never had an office. He worked at a desk on the bank floor, where he met with customers seeking loans. His underwriting consisted primarily of sizing up would-be borrowers, knowing their people, and studying the shine of their shoes. He was rarely wrong.

Daddy Cliff's bank uniform varied little. He wore a gray or blue suit, occasionally a blue blazer. His shirt was invariably white, his tie conservative, his wingtips black or brown. Not much changed after hours. At a holiday gathering my cousins talked him into trying to play tennis at the court behind Aunt Tut and Uncle Bob's house. Daddy Cliff took off his coat, but that was the only change. He neither loosened his tie nor rolled up his sleeves. He was not a casual man.

Daddy Cliff was the bank's president for nearly 20 years, but he and Momie were never wealthy by any means. He had opportunities to head bigger banks in bigger cities, but the two of them decided there was no better place to live than Tupelo. They moved to a small three-bedroom house on Highland Circle when their children were young and lived there the rest of their lives. There was a willow oak in front that was huge by the time I came along and a fig tree next to the utility room in back. The master bedroom doubled as a den. The two adults and four children, and often a member of their extended family living with them, shared a single bathroom that had a bathtub but no shower. There was only one telephone as well, a black rotary phone in the hall. Momie and Daddy Cliff were raised before telephones were common and never learned basic phone etiquette. They answered by saying *alright*, not *hello*, and hung up without saying goodbye when they decided the conversation was over.

Daddy Cliff was elected to Tupelo's City Council, then called the Board of Aldermen, and served six terms, from 1949 to 1973, the same year he retired from the bank. One year the mayor had a heart attack and Daddy Cliff ran both the bank and the city until he recovered. A Tupelo resident seeking a zoning change once suggested to Daddy Cliff that he would move his banking business to the Peoples Bank if he got a favorable decision from the city. Daddy Cliff dismissed him on the spot. For years Daddy Cliff gave the hundred dollars a month he made as an alderman to a widow who had worked at First Methodist Church and was unable to support herself. He also served as president of the Mississippi Bankers Association and helped bring many new businesses to Tupelo. One of the city's principal thoroughfares, Eason Boulevard, is named for him. In all likelihood few who travel it today know who he was or what he did for the city where they live. He died in 1981, during the summer after my second year of law school.

Thirty years after Daddy Cliff died, Daddy came to live with Carrie and me in our home in Ridgeland, a suburb north of Jackson. It was two months before Daddy's 90th birthday and his first change of residence in 55 years. Not long after he got settled, we took him back to Tupelo one weekend to go through his things. Among his papers we found a letter addressed to me from the president of Standard Life Insurance Company informing me that Daddy Cliff had bought a small policy to help pay for my college education. The insurance executive wrote:

You are to be congratulated that you
have a grandfather who has the foresight
and means to plan for your future to
the end that, when the time comes for
you to assume the responsibilities of
manhood, you will be better prepared
and the going will be a little easier.
I am sure that, as time passes, you will
realize more than now the wisdom of your
grandfather's decision.

The letter was dated October 7, 1957. The author did not intend for me to read it immediately. I was just over three months old. Daddy Cliff was planning ahead. Mama and Daddy could have used the insurance policy for its intended purpose, but they didn't. I got a scholarship and earned spending money with summer jobs, Mama and Daddy paid the rest, and I cashed in the policy during my senior year to buy an engagement ring. College was much cheaper in the 1970s than it is today. My tuition at the University of Mississippi, known as Ole Miss, was $351.00 a semester, most of which my scholarship covered. Now it's more than 10 times as much.

Daddy Cliff was the president of the bank, but Momie ruled the roost. Though she was less than five feet tall and weighed 80 pounds, she was in charge. She had a beautiful smile and quick wit and kept everything straight, taking care of the house, the children, and then the grandchildren. There was always ice cream in the freezer.

In 1940 Momie was diagnosed with tuberculosis and spent a year in a sanatorium in south Mississippi. In spite of her illness and the separation, she remained the family matriarch. Also among the papers we discovered in Daddy's house was a stack of letters from Momie written during her time in the sanatorium. Daddy Cliff had saved them. In one she expressed concern that Daddy, then a freshman at Ole Miss, was not focused on his studies. She was more concerned about his attention to his grades than about her loss of a lung. She was not a self-centered woman.

Momie and Daddy Cliff's three oldest children—Daddy, Tut, and Puddie—lived nearly all their adult lives in Tupelo. We gathered at each other's homes for Thanksgiving, Christmas, and the Fourth of July. My favorite place for holiday meals was Tut and Bob's. All the women in the family were good cooks, but Tut was the best and they had not only the tennis court but also a yard big enough for touch football. Tut was also the most stylish of our relatives. She drove a Thunderbird with back doors that opened to the back—so-called suicide doors, fashionable but dangerous—and she poured buttermilk on their brick patio to make the moss grow because she liked the way it looked. I also loved to go to Puddie and Guy's and play with their four children. They had several acres on the edge of town with a tree house and a rope swing hanging from an oak limb 30 feet high. They later added a pool and a tennis court. Puddie taught swimming lessons and was my tennis coach in high school. Tut was one of my kindergarten teachers.

Every year on Easter and Mother's Day Momie and Daddy Cliff took us all to Sunday dinner after church. They would reserve a private room at the Hotel Tupelo or the Rex Plaza for the 15 of us who lived in Tupelo. After Grandma moved back to Tupelo to be near Mama, Momie and Daddy Cliff invited her to join us. Sometimes Doris and her husband Tom Joyner and their children drove up from Jackson. Those of us whose mothers were alive wore red roses on Mother's Day. White roses were worn by those whose mothers were deceased.

On Friday nights Momie and Daddy Cliff sometimes took us to dinner at the Natchez Trace Inn, named for the federal parkway that runs from Nashville, Tennessee, to Natchez, Mississippi, along a route that was carved into the wilderness by Native Americans centuries ago. The Trace passes through Tupelo less than a mile from the home where I grew up on Rogers Drive and is even closer to the home in Ridgeland where Carrie and I live. The two houses are nearly 170 miles apart.

A gregarious man named Junior Hancock owned the Natchez Trace Inn, including the restaurant and adjacent motel and conference center. Peoples Bank had financed the construction. When we walked into the restaurant with Daddy Cliff, Junior would spot us and proclaim in a voice loud enough for everyone to hear that this was the man who had trusted him and loaned him the money to make his dream come true. Daddy Cliff looked mortified. I wondered why he kept taking us there, but I loved the fried oysters.

Chapter 4

In November 1934, in the midst of the Great Depression, President Roosevelt traveled to Mississippi and gave a speech in Tupelo. He remarked on the hope he saw on people's faces and celebrated the success of the Tennessee Valley Authority. Tupelo had started using TVA-generated electricity in March of that year, making it the first TVA city. Harry Brooks was selected from among the many preachers in Tupelo to give the invocation before FDR spoke. I have a photo of the two of them on the platform. The president, in spite of his polio, is standing.

Nearly a year later, in response to a request from Roosevelt to clergymen throughout the country for an assessment of the nation's recovery from the Depression, Dr. Brooks made a request of his own. The Works Progress Administration had just been established and he urged the president to expand eligibility for the program. In his letter, an excerpt of which appears in a history of FDR's presidency, Dr. Brooks wrote:

```
The Works Program meets a general need,
but there's a pretty general criticism
of it that it applies only for those
who have been on relief rolls. There
are hundreds and thousands of people who
have not asked the government for one
penny of help. Some of them have nothing
scarcely to live upon. Others have but
little, but out of their self-respect
```

and regard for the government of our
nation they have not asked for anything.
These are in need. I personally feel
that they ought to be included in the
Works Program.

Dr. Brooks wrote about a tragedy of a different sort the following year. After dark on Sunday evening, April 5, 1936, Daddy Cliff's 38th birthday, a massive tornado struck Tupelo without warning. More than 200 residents were killed, perhaps far more. The precise number is unknown because many were in the poor black section of town and were not included in the death toll. In addition to the fatalities, at least 700 people were injured. The tornado leveled 48 city blocks and destroyed hundreds of homes. Every member of a family of 13 was killed. The tornado remains the fourth deadliest in the nation's history.

My parents and their families escaped from the devastation unhurt. Mama and Daddy, who were in the ninth grade, were both at home when the tornado struck. Sunday evening services over, the Brooks family had returned to the parsonage. Two weeks after the storm Dr. Brooks described what they witnessed.

The church services had been dismissed,
the people generally had returned home
and were quietly reading or having con-
verse about their home altars, some had
retired, others were driving in their
cars. This pastor had had a meeting with
his choir leader and organist, arrang-
ing and talking over the arrangements
for Holy Week and Easter Sunday morning,
also a meeting with Mr. W. L. Elkin,
the Superintendent of his Church School,
planning a week of instruction for a
class of Church School children, who
were to be received into the membership

of the Church on Easter Sunday morning. He had just gotten to the parsonage porch, he looked to the west, the sky was black with clouds, and the southwest was aflame with fire coming this way. For a few moments, there was a deathless stillness, then a roar of wind that sounded like the rumble of a thousand freight cars on tracks irregularly constructed. The electric lights went out; inside the house a fearful expectancy possessed our minds and hearts. Mrs. Brooks and the children joined me in the central east room. The house shook like a large plate of Jell-O suddenly turned on a plate. A crash broke upon the house—a huge oak had fallen on the roof. When we emerged from the house, the rain began to come in torrents. The lawns all around us were full of trees fallen. Some of them had stood for years. Shingles, chairs, porch chairs, bricks, porch pillars, everything lay in the streets and lawns everywhere.

We hurried across the street to a seeming place of safety. There were no lights anywhere, the sky was black with clouds. Soon we began to hear the cries for help. Trees and debris filled the streets to the west and north, men came carrying on improvised carts the wounded, others came leading their maimed, still others carrying them on their shoulders, others carrying children and babies in their arms, to the hospital, and when the rain began to pour through the roof,

```
then the march turned toward the annex
of the Methodist Church, when that was
filled, then into the dry spots in the
parsonage, and then to the courthouse
and the Lyric Theater. The City Hall
became a morgue where the dead were
placed for identification.
```

The home on Highland Circle where the Easons lived was farther than the parsonage from the path of the storm. The family had finished Daddy Cliff's birthday dinner when the tornado passed to the east. After the worst was over, Daddy Cliff and Daddy went outside to survey the damage. As they headed east on Jackson Street, lightning lit up the sky. Church Street School, where Daddy had attended elementary school, was no longer standing. Most of it was gone altogether and the rest reduced to rubble. They walked downtown to the hospital to see what they could do to help. A woman they knew had been strapped to a door to stabilize her broken back and screamed as she was carried up a flight of stairs.

The tornado destroyed much of Tupelo. Almost 15 percent of its 7,000 residents were killed or injured and many more were left homeless. But Harry Brooks still found reason for hope.

```
Some readers may be wondering, how
are the people coming back? Never have
I seen a people more heroic than these.
Noble sons and daughters of the city
beautiful. Husbands and wives separated
for years have been brought together,
enemies have met and joined in friend-
ship, men estranged from God and their
churches have rededicated themselves.
This last Sunday, we met for worship
in theaters, the courthouse, and in
churches not destroyed. The people came
by the hundreds, yea by the thousands,
```

and filled every house with anxious wor-
shipers. The people's minds and hearts
are turned to God.

Some beautiful lessons on devotion
and faith are coming out from under the
wreckage of homes. In one place, the
house was blown over and into a com-
pletely wrecked state. The mother was
under the ruins but was able to extri-
cate herself. She was much bruised and
bleeding, but she began a search for
her children. She found them all but
her eight- or ten-month-old baby. She
sought it everywhere but could not find
it, when suddenly she heard the howl of
the family bulldog, a faithful guardian
and play fellow of the children. When
she found him under the debris, he was
bruised and bleeding, and underneath him
lay her baby, its clothes covered with
the blood of the faithful heroic dog, but
not one scratch of injury on the baby.
Both mother and dog have been treated
for their injuries and are recovering.

Dr. Brooks had written FDR about the WPA the year before
the storm. The year after, the WPA built a new school on Church
Street where the old one had been. A scale model of the Art Deco
building was displayed at the World's Fair in New York City in 1939.

My children always give me books for Christmas. In 2018 Ann
Lowrey gave me an excellent novel called *Promise* based on the
experiences during the 1936 tornado of two fictional families in
Tupelo, one white and one black. While reading it, I learned that
the author, Minrose Gwin, had grown up in Tupelo and was an
English professor at the University of North Carolina. I thought
she might be interested in what Dr. Brooks had written about the

storm, so I found her email address and sent it to her. I also said she might have known my parents and grandparents and told her who they were. She thanked me and said Mama must have been one of the Brooks twins and that her mother, Erin Taylor Clayton, had loved them both dearly. I asked if her mother's nickname was Tatie and she confirmed that it was. I remember her well. She said Tatie, who was in the ninth grade with Mama and Daddy at the time of the tornado, lived on Church Street. Fortunately for Minrose, who was born a decade later, Tatie fared better than the school did.

Several months after my email exchange with Minrose, I was going through old family pictures and came across a photo of her grandparents' home taken immediately after the storm. It was one of very few on Church Street that was still standing. I emailed a copy of the photo to Minrose. She had written a novel about the tornado but had never seen the picture.

Chapter 5

In 1938, the year Julie Francis was born in Tulsa, Harry Brooks was transferred to Greenwood, 125 miles southwest of Tupelo, where he served as the Superintendent of the Greenwood District of the North Mississippi Methodist Conference. The twins stayed behind to finish their senior year, living with a friend and her family and graduating along with Daddy from Tupelo High School in 1939. In September the three started college, Daddy in Oxford at Ole Miss and Mama and Marjory in Columbus at Mississippi State College for Women, known as MSCW or simply the W. All three thrived during their years in college. Daddy was elected president of his fraternity and the twins were named Most Versatile and chosen for the MSCW Hall of Fame.

The same month they started college, Great Britain and France declared war on Germany in response to its invasion of Poland, and World War II began in Europe. With American involvement becoming more likely with each passing month, Daddy made plans to serve as a pilot in the Navy. After Christmas break his freshman year he scraped together $25 and bought an old Model T Ford with no top—the kind with a crank in the front that has to be wound to start the engine—and drove it to the Oxford airport for flying lessons so he would have his pilot's license when the time came. He had just turned 18 but was already doing the right thing.

The war spread during the next two years, but the United States was able to stay out of it. That came to an abrupt end on December 7, 1941, when the Japanese bombed Pearl Harbor. America declared war on Japan the next day, and Germany and its Axis partners declared war on America less than a week later. After Pearl Harbor Daddy increased his course load and went to summer school so he could finish early and join the Naval Air Corps. He graduated in December 1942, a semester ahead of the rest of his class. Also in December Harry Brooks died of cancer in Greenwood. He was buried beside Grandma's parents in Carlton, Texas.

According to his gravestone, Dr. Brooks was born on December 29, 1875. If he had really been born then, that would mean he died right before his 67th birthday. While making final revisions to the manuscript for this book, however, I learned that he was actually born much earlier and was thus much older. But that's a story for later in the book.

Daddy wanted to serve in the Pacific, but his skills as a pilot kept him in the States. He excelled in flight school and the Navy made him a flight instructor. He appealed the decision and pressed his case to a board of officers but was unsuccessful. Nearly 60 years later he described himself as crazy but lucky—crazy for wanting to fight in the Pacific, lucky because they turned him down. So instead of flying combat missions, Daddy trained other pilots who did. He was on a training flight over Atlanta in August 1945 when word came over the radio that the Enola Gay had dropped a weapon called an atomic bomb on the Japanese city of Hiroshima. The pilot at the controls on the training flight banked into a turn, headed back to the base, and landed. When asked why he cut the flight short, he declared with confidence that the war was over. He was wrong but not by much. A second bomb was dropped on Nagasaki three days later, and Emperor Hirohito announced Japan's surrender less than a week after that.

Hundreds of thousands of young men in Daddy's generation were not as lucky as he was. The younger Sidney Davis was also a pilot in World War II. He was in the Army Air Corps, later to become the Air Force, and flew in Europe. He was shot down and killed near the end of the war on a flight over the Adriatic Sea off the eastern shore of Italy. His survivors included a widow in her twenties and two young daughters. Among the other family members he left behind were his older sister Betty Davis Francis and his niece Julie, who was six.

Another of the unlucky ones was Louis Benoist, a dear friend and fraternity brother of Daddy's from Natchez. Among Daddy's papers I found three letters from Louis and a fourth one about him.

Louis wrote the first letter less than a week after D-Day while he was in basic training at Camp Shelby in south Mississippi. He reported to Daddy that he had learned to fall asleep wherever he hit the ground—"it can be done; I do it." He said he hadn't taken a bath in Lord knows when and his last one was in a swamp where he "had to beat the snakes off in order to make room for me."

Louis sent the second letter six weeks later from Fort George Meade in Maryland and wrote that he might be quite some distance away by the time Daddy read it. Louis had just been ordered to go overseas, which was unfortunate because his wife Anne was expecting their first child in a matter of days. But Louis added optimistically that things could be worse, that Anne was in good hands and would be well taken care of.

The last letter in Daddy's papers that Louis wrote, and perhaps the last one he ever wrote, was to Daddy's sister Myra, who was Tut to us, congratulating her on her recent marriage to Bob Leake. Louis expressed the view that marriage was a wonderful institution and wrote of how much he would love to be home with his wife, who had given birth to their son shortly after he shipped out to Europe. But he couldn't be home in Mississippi with his wife and son because it was January 1945 and he was in Belgium fighting the Germans in the Battle of the Bulge. The night before, he wrote, he'd been trapped in his foxhole by eight inches of snow and had to yell for his men to free him. Fortunately they got there before the Germans did. He said he hoped to keep on dodging fire from the German 88s, antitank guns—"they say people can get hurt with those things"—and thanked Myra for a letter she had sent him. He also asked her to write again. "Letters from home are all we look forward to. War is so very horrible and ugly that it gets you down. Letters are the only thing I know of which helps to obliterate the horrors."

The fourth letter I found was to Daddy from Louis's widow Anne. Louis had been killed in action in Germany less than four weeks after sending the letter of congratulations to Myra. Anne reported that he was cut down by German machine gun fire leading his platoon up a hill through a wooded area, their advance hampered by the deep snow. Louis had promised Anne he wasn't going to be a hero, but he died a hero, leading his men into battle. She included several sentences in her letter that may have been as much for her own benefit as for Daddy's. "You know, Paul, Louis loved you deeply, and to know that will always prove to be a comfort. He was happy while he was married and terribly proud to have a son. I adored him and he knew it, and I know that he adored me." Louis was killed while they were taking Hoffman, Germany, a place Anne wrote that "isn't even on the map."

When I showed the letters to Carrie, she suggested that I track down Louis's family and send the letters to them. With an internet search and several emails, I got the address for Louis's son, Louis Benoist IV, and mailed the letters to him. He was the baby who came into the world only months before the father who never met him left it, but he was now 74 and had recently retired from a long and successful career as an orthopedic surgeon. He lived in Amarillo, Texas, where Mama was born. His daughter Marie put me in touch with French Maclean of Decatur, Illinois, a retired colonel who was writing a book about the losses suffered by the infantrymen of Company B in World War II. French told me that his dad, Mac Maclean, had served in Louis's platoon and thought the world of him. French also told me that the correct name of the village Louis was killed trying to take was Höfen, not Hoffman as Anne had been told. It's little wonder she couldn't find it on the map.

The closest Daddy came to getting shot by the enemy was in Mississippi after the war was over. When he was discharged from the Navy in the summer of 1946, jobs were scarce, so he took advantage of the GI Bill and returned to Ole Miss to make up for the semester he'd missed by graduating early. When asked many years later what he studied, he said "campusology." Not long ago a friend sent me a photo of his dad and mine playing poker at the fraternity house that fall. I never saw Daddy do anything more sinful.

Returning in the fall gave Daddy a chance to be in Oxford for one more Ole Miss football season. During the week before the final game of the year against Mississippi State, Daddy and several other veterans drove to Tupelo, rented planes, and flew south to Starkville to drop leaflets on the enemy campus. Several weeks later, when Daddy returned to the Tupelo airport, an official had a surprise to show him: There were bullet holes in one of the planes. As the pilots had swooped low over the campus, someone, almost certainly another veteran, had opened fire. Adding insult to injury, Mississippi State won the game easily, 20–0.

Because Daddy's make-up semester was in the fall and the one he missed was in the spring, he got to spend five football seasons in Oxford. Ole Miss lost to Mississippi State all five years, in '39 through '42 and again in '46. Because of the war neither school fielded a team in 1943, but Ole Miss won the games in both '44 and '45. In 1947, the year after Daddy's final semester, Johnny Vaught took over as the head coach in Oxford and Ole Miss started winning again. In Vaught's first 10 games against the in-state rival, the Rebels won nine times. The 1953 game ended in a tie. Of the 17 games between 1939 and 1956, Ole Miss lost only five, but they were the five when Daddy was in school there. He was only auditing classes in the fall of '46 and didn't stick around for final exams. After seeing Ole Miss lose to State for the last time, with football season over, Daddy went home to Tupelo and got a job.

Chapter 6

Daddy's first position after his post-war semester at Ole Miss was in the accounting department at McCarty Holman, which owned the chain of Jitney Jungle grocery stores in Mississippi and neighboring states. Daddy worked six days a week, 10 hours a day, and lived with Momie and Daddy Cliff on Highland Circle while he saved money to get a car and a place of his own. I don't know what became of the $25 Model T Ford, but he must have sold it or given it away. Daddy had missed Momie's cooking during the years since he'd left for college and enjoyed being back home.

Daddy had been a member of Boy Scout Troop 12 as a teenager. In 1939 he achieved the highest rank in Scouting, becoming only the fifth Eagle Scout since the troop's inception more than a decade earlier. He came home one weekend during his first semester at Ole Miss to receive the award.

After returning to Tupelo for good seven years later, Daddy was walking home from work one evening when Troop 12 Scoutmaster A. P. Bennett saw him and stopped to talk. Bennett, who was also the high school principal, said he was busy with school and needed some help with the troop. To convince Daddy to volunteer, Bennett assured him it would be for just a few months. In describing the conversation with the benefit of hindsight more than half a century later, Daddy said, "but you know how that goes."

Despite his 60-hour-a-week work schedule, Daddy agreed to help. Bennett soon saw that the troop was in good hands and bowed out. Daddy was less than a decade older than many of the boys, but he had served in the Navy during the war and they respected him.

He also impressed them with his physical fitness. One of Daddy's first Scouts told me many years later that he amazed them by doing push-ups with one arm.

Daddy had agreed to help with the troop for just a few months, but before he was finished the few months had stretched into more than 700. He served as the head Scoutmaster of Troop 12 for 45 years, then as an assistant for another 15. He worked and camped with the troop from his mid-twenties to his mid-eighties. He was a young man physically until he was very old. He hiked 24 miles from the North Rim to the South Rim of the Grand Canyon shortly before his 70th birthday and 14 miles up and down the steep hills of the Civil War battlefield at Vicksburg the month he turned 81.

Daddy had already been the leader of Troop 12 nearly three years when he married Mama. Less than six months after the wedding he took a group of boys to the national Boy Scout jamboree in Valley Forge, Pennsylvania. One of the boys on the trip told me decades later that Daddy had rented a plane and taken them up for an aerial tour of the jamboree site. They looked down on the grounds where nearly 50,000 boys were camping and on the Delaware River where George Washington made his famous crossing on Christmas night in 1776 to attack the Hessian forces in Trenton, New Jersey.

One of Daddy's first Eagle Scouts was an outstanding young man named Ken Kirk. Ken later served as co-captain of the 1959 Ole Miss football team, which gave up only 21 points the entire season and won the national championship. He then played for the Bears, Steelers, and Rams in the NFL. A suggestion Ken made a decade earlier, however, had a greater impact on more people than anything he accomplished on a football field.

Ken made the suggestion on a campout in 1951 when he was a member of Troop 12. While he and Daddy were sitting by a campfire, he said that camping was the best thing about Scouting. The troop, he continued, should go every month. Daddy thought it over, agreed, and in August of that year Troop 12 began a tradition of going on at least one overnight camping trip every single month. Since then, no matter the weather, the troop has never missed. Other than when Mama was sick and he needed to stay home with her, Daddy never missed either until he finally got too old to go. During his six decades as a leader of the troop, he spent more than three years' worth of nights—more than a thousand altogether—sleeping on the ground in a tent.

Ken died in 2009 and Daddy died four years later, but the practice that started with Ken's suggestion has outlived them both. In March 2018 Troop 12 camped for the 800th month in a row. Four months later the unbroken streak reached 67 years. The tradition that began during the Korean War had spanned 13 presidencies, from Truman to Trump.

Although Mama learned in the first years of their marriage how much time Daddy devoted to Troop 12, she did not know how long his devotion would last. Until her final illness, from which she died in 1999 at 78, Daddy was still camping with the troop every month. Half a century earlier, when Daddy proposed to her, she could not have known he would be a Boy Scout leader for the entire length of their marriage and the rest of her life. He could not have known either.

Chapter 7

In 1947, the same year Daddy became Troop 12's Scoutmaster, Betty Davis Francis married for the second time. Her groom was Herb Smith, the president of Sinclair Oil Company. Herb was a self-made man. He had little formal education but was a genius at finding oil. He was 23 years older than his bride and only two years younger than his new father-in-law Sidney Davis. Herb was born in February 1889 and, like Paul Mims Eason, had fought in France in World War I.

Herb was a widower; his wife Miriam had died suddenly of a cerebral hemorrhage. They had three sons and a daughter named Sandy, their youngest. When Betty and Julie joined the family, Sandy got the sister she'd always wanted. The two were close in age and shared a bedroom. With the house full of older boys, the girls formed an alliance and maintained a very close relationship even after they grew up, got married, and lived far apart. More than 70 years after her father married Julie's mother, Sandy told Carrie and me how much she loved Julie.

Two years after Herb and Betty married, she gave birth to their only child and his fourth son. But Herb didn't get to the hospital in time and his tardiness cost him naming privileges. When he arrived, he was greeted by his father-in-law, who announced that he was too late, the child had already been born and already been named. Herb learned that his new son was Sidney Davis Smith from Sidney Hugh Davis, who got there first. The baby, called Sid, was more than a decade younger than his two half-sisters and 60 years younger than his father. Like Daddy, he has the same first name as an uncle who was killed in a world war just a few years before he was born.

Five months after Sid was born, his grandmother Minnie passed away. His grandfather did not remain alone for long. In the following year, 1950, Sidney Davis married Louise Hanks, a widow with two children. Louise was 15 years younger than Sidney, closer in age to her new step-daughter than to her husband and more than a decade younger than her new son-in-law.

Chapter 8

Mama and Daddy also got married in 1950, on January 21 in Tupelo. I know nothing about their courtship or their wedding or even what led Mama to move back to Tupelo. I wish I had asked, just as I wish I had asked them many other things. But I was too much like the son in Harry Chapin's "Cat's in the Cradle," too caught up in my own life to ask them about theirs.

Several years ago Carrie and I went with a group of friends to San Miguel, the beautiful, historic city in central Mexico. We were there for the Day of the Dead, the ritual that has been celebrated since long before the birth of Christ. Around El Jardin, the central plaza and the site of La Parroquia de San Miguel Arcángel, the magnificent parish church built in the 1800s, residents had erected elaborate altars to their deceased loved ones. One of the altars included an empty tequila bottle. We visited the city's principal cemetery, which is elaborately decorated for the occasion each year. Families clean and place marigolds on the graves of their ancestors and stay there through the night on November 1 telling stories about them. Spending the night in a cemetery may seem ghoulish, but it's a wonderful way to keep family history and stories alive. We have no similar practice in America and many family stories, like the story of the romance that led to my parents' marriage, are lost in the mists of time.

So I don't know why Mama came back to Tupelo, but I don't believe it was because of Daddy. I know they didn't date in high school and they couldn't have dated in college or when Daddy was in the Navy. Not only were they far apart, but Daddy was not the dating type. Years later he said he never went out on a date unless he was forced. Daddy was handsome but shy. He was also the straightest of arrows. Other than a single glass of champagne on holidays, he hardly ever drank. I was shocked when he ordered a beer at dinner one night when we were on vacation at the beach. I never saw him drink another one until long after I was grown. When I came to Tupelo to see him in his later years, there would be a six-pack of my favorite, Samuel Adams Boston Lager, waiting in the refrigerator. He would drink one beer with me, occasionally two, never three. If I didn't drink all the others, they would still be there the next time I came.

My older sister and only sibling was born in June 1955. My parents chose two family names, christening her Margaret Ethel Eason. I don't know if she was named Margaret for Momie or for Mama—that's another question I never asked—though she could have been named for both. To avoid confusion with the two of them, they called her Margie and, to avoid confusion with Marjory, they pronounced Margie with a hard g.

The year after Margie was born, Mama and Daddy bought the small three-bedroom home on Rogers Drive. The house was new; it had been built by their brother-in-law Bob Leake, Tut's husband. In a conversation nearly 50 years later Daddy claimed he agreed with Bob on the price before he and Mama ever set foot in the house. Maybe he and Bob settled on the amount, but I doubt that Daddy made a firm commitment to buy the house without Mama's blessing. That would not have been like him. But if he did, that means Mama had nothing to say about the purchase of their one and only home. Over the years they talked about building another house—they even picked out a lot and hired a designer to draft plans—but for some reason they never did. They lived on Rogers Drive until Mama died there 43 years after they moved in. Daddy stayed another dozen years until he got too old to live alone and came to Ridgeland to live with Carrie and me.

After Daddy moved in with us in September 2011, we sold his house but only after I laid claim to the closet door in the bedroom that had been mine until I left for college 36 years earlier. By then the door was covered not just with lines marking Margie's height and mine as we grew taller but another set of lines for the six children in the next generation—Margie's three and my three—that were made on our trips home to Tupelo. There were also lines on the bottom half of the door for my first three grandchildren. Now the door hangs on a wall in our home and lines for all four of my grandchildren are making their way up the door. One day I noticed two lines that were close together. The name and date beside one were in Mama's handwriting, the name and date beside the other in mine. Mama had measured me on the Fourth of July in 1964, the day after I turned seven. I had measured my oldest grandchild on June 18, 2011, the day after she turned seven. I was taller by a quarter of an inch.

Chapter 9

Julie graduated from high school in Tulsa in 1956, the same year my parents bought their first and last home. Julie was very bright and had many options for college. She chose Washington University in St. Louis. It was 400 miles from home, far enough away but not too far. In 1960, 50 years after her grandparents had married in the same city, Julie graduated with a degree in liberal arts. By all accounts she was a good student and very popular with her classmates.

Late the following year Sidney Davis, then 75, decided he needed a new estate plan. He wanted to provide for his second wife Louise, who was 15 years younger than he was and almost certain to outlive him, but he wanted the bulk of his assets to go to his children and grandchildren, not hers. He requested his lawyer, Fenelon Boesche of Tulsa, to prepare a new will reflecting his wishes.

The will, which Sidney signed in January 1962, split the bulk of his substantial holdings into four equal parts, one for Louise and one for each of his three surviving children, Betty, Roger, and William. The children were to receive some properties outright, principally oil and gas wells in Louisiana, but most of the assets would be placed in separate trusts for their benefit. The trusts were designed to outlive them. When one died, the trust for that child's benefit would be split into separate trusts for the child's children—Sidney's grandchildren—with the income to be distributed quarterly and the principal to be distributed in three equal shares on the grandchild's 25th, 30th, and 40th birthdays.

The trust for each grandchild was to terminate with the final principal distribution at age 40, but the will contained a provision to deal with the remote possibility than a grandchild might die before reaching 40. If a grandchild had already passed away when it came time to make any of the three distributions of principal, the will directed that the trust would terminate immediately and all the assets would be distributed to the grandchild's "issue," a legal term for child or children. The clause made Sidney's great-grandchildren potential beneficiaries of his will.

Chapter 10

Julie returned to Tulsa after she graduated from Washington University in 1960, but Tulsa was no St. Louis and she soon grew bored. She wanted something bigger and she wanted something new. Brenda Boone, a high school classmate who had stayed in Oklahoma for college and was also back in Tulsa, felt the same way. The two decided to move to Denver and get a place together. They rented an apartment on Vine Street. During her time in Denver Julie worked as a travel agent. She had gone on many family trips when she was growing up and loved to travel and loved the job. It was the only real job she ever had.

During her time at the agency Julie won a sailing trip in the Caribbean. She wasn't dating anyone at the time and called a college friend, Lewis Bettman, who was also her financial advisor, and asked him to join her. At the time Lewis was involved in a battle for control of the St. Louis Young Republicans. He would miss a key vote if he went sailing so he turned her down. Fifty-five years later he wondered what he could have been thinking, choosing a political fight over a sailing trip with Julie.

While she was living in Denver, Julie appeared from the outside to have it all. She was smart as a whip according to one contemporary and was also stylish, sophisticated, and beautiful. Friends often remarked that she bore a striking resemblance to Elizabeth Taylor, only with lighter hair. And Julie's family was wealthy, which gave her freedom. Freedom to stock up on the latest fashions, freedom to travel whenever and wherever she wanted, freedom from worry about how to support herself and pay her bills.

But that was from the outside. On the inside something was missing. Julie would dress up, go out, and have fun, but she never seemed truly happy. According to Brenda there was always a sadness about her. And she drank too much. She had drunk too much in college, but most everybody drank a lot then. Julie still did.

While she was living with Brenda, Julie met Lee Farnham, who had graduated from Middlebury College in Vermont in 1960 and worked for Pan American World Airways in Denver. The two began dating, fell in love, and got engaged. They married in Tulsa on April 18, 1964. Both were 25. They were an attractive couple and appeared headed for a happy and successful life together.

Lee assumed Julie's family had money but had no idea how much. He first suspected they were truly wealthy when Sidney Davis informed him that a prenuptial agreement would have to be executed before the wedding. If Lee and Julie divorced, the agreement provided that he would receive $25,000 but would otherwise make no claim on her assets or income. Sidney was a generous man, but he wanted to keep the money in the family. Prenuptial agreements for 25-year-old travel agents are rare now but were almost unheard of then.

After the wedding the newlyweds returned to Denver. They did not go on a honeymoon immediately, so Lee returned to work. When he got home to their apartment after his first day back on the job, he found it filled with new furniture, which Julie declared was her wedding present to him. More than half a century later he still had some of the furniture he came home to in Denver that day.

The following year Lee was transferred to Salt Lake City, where Pan Am did significant business with the Church of Jesus Christ of Latter-day Saints. Julie enjoyed some things about life in Utah —she attended the ballet and opera and loved the mountains—but on the whole she was not happy. She liked to smoke and she really liked to drink, and both habits put her at odds with the straitlaced culture dominated by the Mormon Church. She found it stifling. Julie also missed her job as a travel agent. She was unable to work in a similar position in Salt Lake City because Lee's new boss at Pan Am regarded it as a conflict of interest.

Julie had received a Siamese cat as a wedding present that she named Taj. Beginning during their years in Salt Lake City the couple tried to start a family. When their efforts proved to be futile, they expanded the family by acquiring more Siamese cats to keep both them and Taj company. They wound up with four altogether and loved them all.

While Lee and Julie were living in Utah, Sidney Davis took them and his entire extended family to Hawaii one Christmas. On another occasion Julie's father Tom Francis and his second wife Jane came from New York to Salt Lake City for a visit. Jane had been Tom's nurse when he was recovering from polio and the two reunited after Tom and Betty divorced. After spending time with Lee and Julie, Tom and Jane drove east to Aspen. Tom was wheelchair-bound, his health was poor, and the high altitude of Aspen was too much for him. He suffered a massive heart attack. He was rushed down to the lower elevation of Denver but didn't make it. He was only 56.

Not long after the funeral Lee was scheduled for an extended business trip to Europe to focus on Pan Am's ties to Mormon missions there. Julie planned to go with him and they asked Jane to join them so she would have something to take her mind off her husband's sudden death.

During the trip Jane decided to stay behind in Paris while Lee and Julie went on to England. But Jane didn't remain in Paris. Instead she returned to their previous stop, Lausanne, Switzerland, to reunite with a man she had met there who was a friend of Lee's family. The two left Lausanne together and next surfaced back in the States, where they had gone to Reno for the man to divorce his wife and marry Jane. She was not a grieving widow for long.

Lee was fluent in Spanish and after two years in Utah was offered an opportunity to transfer to a management position with Pan Am in South America. He and Julie first visited La Paz, Bolivia, but Julie didn't like it so they settled on Cali, Colombia. Lee still didn't have a full grasp of the extent of Julie's wealth and never did, but he got a sense of it during their time in Cali. One day he saw a statement for the dividends she received from a single stock,

Standard Oil of California, and the amount exceeded his annual salary at Pan Am. But he was still the breadwinner. They lived on his salary; other than for trips and special purchases, she reinvested her interest and dividends.

At their home in Cali the couple had a cook, housekeeper, and gardener, and Julie lived a life of leisure. The living was easy, but it wasn't healthy. Lee was often away on business, Julie had little to do, and she didn't speak the language. So she drank. It was during her time in Colombia that Julie's drinking spiraled out of control. In a sense Julie became a captive of the bottle because she could. At an age when most women are raising children or holding jobs or both, Julie did neither. So instead of getting ready for work or making breakfast for her family, Julie made herself a drink. Her freedom—freedom from the demands of a family and a job—proved to be a trap. There is dignity in work. It gives a person discipline and purpose. Having to work or raise a family might have given Julie purpose and it might have altered the course of her life.

After nearly three years in Colombia Lee accepted a position in Mexico City with the U.S. Travel Service, a Commerce Department agency created in 1961 to encourage tourists from foreign countries to visit America. Julie, who had been at home with her family for the Christmas holidays, drove their Volkswagen station wagon from Tulsa to Mexico City in January 1970. There she and Lee spent their last month together. Julie was tired of living in a foreign country where the people spoke a language that was foreign to her. She had declined to take Spanish lessons and, even after her years in Cali, was still not fluent. And Lee would now have responsibility for 20 countries and be gone most of the time. Julie would be on her own.

They talked it over. There was little anger in their marriage and there had been good times. Because Lee was a manager at Pan Am, they were able to fly all over the world—to Europe, Australia, Hawaii, and elsewhere. They met a couple who ran a resort in Antigua and flew to see them several times. The two couples took overnight sailing trips from Antigua to Barbuda, which was still uninhabited. The boat would anchor offshore and the crew would rig a charcoal grill on the rail and cook the fish caught along the way. The stars, the ocean breeze, and the company of good friends made for a wonderful time.

But in the end, despite the good times, there was not enough to keep Julie and Lee together. Perhaps children would have made a difference, but they had not succeeded in having any. So they agreed to go their separate ways and divided their belongings. Lee took Julie to the Mexico City airport and felt numb as she boarded the plane and their cats were loaded into the baggage compartment in their kennels. Julie returned home to Tulsa, as she did time and again, and moved back in with Betty. It was just the two of them. By then Betty and Herb had also divorced, and Sid was away at college. Not long after Julie arrived, Lee drove the Volkswagen back to Tulsa and delivered it to Julie, slept in a separate bedroom, then flew back to Mexico City alone.

The divorce was finalized quickly. They had been married only six years but stayed in touch after their marriage ended for much longer than that. Lee would call to check on Julie and the cats—many years later he recalled the sweet note she sent him when Taj died—and they exchanged Christmas cards every year. Until the year he sent a card but she did not.

After her return from Cali Julie saw a number of friends she had not seen during her years in South America. They were shocked by her appearance. One of them hardly recognized her and concluded that she had been ravaged by alcohol. Another observed that the combination of sun and drink had left her skin looking like a coconut.

Julie reluctantly came to grips with the fact that she had a drinking problem. She turned for help to Lewis Bettman, who arranged for her to be admitted to Silver Hill Foundation in Connecticut, the same facility where Ted Kennedy's wife, Joan, was treated. It was the first of a handful of stints in rehab. Years later Julie wrote Lewis a note to express her appreciation. "For the zillionth time, I thank you again for your friendship and support in my efforts to lick my damn problem." She never did.

Chapter 11

Mama and Marjory, who had studied chemistry and bacteriology at MSCW, moved to Lake Charles, Louisiana, after graduation to work in the lab at a chemical plant. When they returned to Tupelo several years later, Mama got a job at the county health department taking and analyzing blood samples, and Marjory taught at the same junior high school she and Mama had attended and I would attend two decades later. Marjory had a boy in her class one year who was unforgettable not because he studied hard or made good grades but because he was strikingly handsome and brought his guitar to school nearly every day. The boy was Elvis Presley.

After Mama and Daddy got married, Marjory decided to leave Tupelo and continue her education. She enjoyed teaching more than working in the lab and got a Master's degree in education at the University of Idaho, which was more than 2,000 miles from Tupelo. She then accepted a teaching position at Ohio State, continued her studies there, and obtained a PhD in psychology. Like her father before her, Marjory was now Dr. Brooks. She spent the rest of her career as a professor and leader at universities around the country, chairing the departments of home economics at Montana State, the University of Maryland, and New Mexico State. She never married.

Marjory was not the usual home economics type. When she accepted the position at New Mexico State in Las Cruces in 1973, where she became the only woman to head an academic department, she confessed to a reporter from the *Albuquerque Journal* that she could neither cook nor sew and had never done either one. She was more interested in encouraging women to take leading roles in universities. She told the reporter: "I don't know why women have to take the back seat in academia. It's all based on tradition and the way little boys and girls are taught about their roles."

Daddy had also changed jobs, but he didn't leave Tupelo. He didn't like his work as an accountant at McCarty Holman and took a position at a plant that made children's clothes. His new employer, Milam Manufacturing Company, was owned by the Milam family of Tupelo. His boss was Gartrell Milam. Daddy was honest and hard-working, treated people with respect, and after several years Gartrell promoted him to the position of plant manager. He no longer worked 60-hour weeks and he got two weeks of vacation when the plant shut down, one week at Christmas and one over the Fourth of July. During his week off in the summer we often took long road trips to wherever Marjory was teaching at the time. The trips allowed us to see America and the twins to see each other. We never flew. Buying four plane tickets would have been out of the question.

Daddy had what appeared to be a good, stable job, but in 1965 the Milams decided to sell their plant and the buyer decided to close it down and relocate the operations to an existing plant in Georgia. Daddy was an able manager and had offers to run facilities in other cities, but that would have meant leaving Tupelo and our friends and relatives, the First Methodist Church, and Troop 12. Daddy was never motivated by money or material things and he and Mama chose to stay in Tupelo. Like Momie and Daddy Cliff, they decided there was no better place to live. From then until he retired two decades later, Daddy was underemployed. It never seemed to bother him, though he wasn't a complainer and would have kept it to himself if it did.

Daddy's first position after leaving Milam was as a purchaser at another clothing plant, this one in Mantachie, a small town east of Tupelo. Before his first day on the job we took our longest road trip ever, a two-week vacation to the West to see the sights and visit Marjory in Bozeman, where she chaired the home economics department at Montana State. It was the first time Daddy had been off work for two weeks in a row in my lifetime.

The trip was more than half a century ago, but I still remember it well. I sat in the middle of the front seat of our station wagon between Mama and Daddy while Margie slept in the back. I was more curious than she was, I'm sure more annoying as well. I questioned Mama and Daddy about everything we saw and identified birds we didn't have in Mississippi with the aid of a Roger Tory Peterson field guide. We went to my first ever major league baseball game in Kansas City and toured Dodge City and Boot Hill in Kansas. I was fascinated by Dodge City because of our Saturday night ritual watching Marshal Dillon, Miss Kitty, Festus, and Doc on *Gunsmoke*, which was Daddy's favorite television show. CBS later moved the show to Monday night, which meant Daddy had to give up one of the few things he did just for himself. Troop 12 met on Monday night. There was no way to record TV shows in the 1960s, so there was no more *Gunsmoke* for him.

After leaving Kansas we continued west to Colorado, where we toured the Air Force Academy and drove to the top of Pikes Peak. In Wyoming the Tetons came into view when they were still far to the west. We camped in Yellowstone with snow on the ground on my eighth birthday, watched Old Faithful erupt right on time, and saw at least a dozen bears. I had the most fun and Mama the least. She didn't like to camp, especially in bear country, and she told me years later she was afraid I would fall into a geyser because I was too excited to watch where I was going. The day after my birthday we continued north to Bozeman and shivered through a fireworks show with Marjory. It's been more than 50 years since then, but I've never been cold on the Fourth of July again. On the way home we toured the Little Big Horn battlefield in southeast Montana, then drove through the Black Hills and Badlands and visited Mount Rushmore in South Dakota. The trip was my first time to see real mountains and it was a revelation. I have made many trips to the mountains of the West since the summer of 1965. I've even written a book about them.

Marjory also made frequent visits to Tupelo, often at Christmas, and I loved spending time with her. She told great stories about her travels and talked to me like I was an adult. She was more friend than parent and made me feel grown up. Nights were worse than days. She slept on the top bunk in my room and snored all night. I wondered how such a little woman could make so much noise.

Grandma moved back to Tupelo when I was young and lived in a small house on Blair Street with a pecan tree in back and a carport on the side that I helped Daddy reroof. Her sisters, including Grace, identical twins Hattie and Carrie, and Irene from Tulsa, whom we called Aunt Idy, came to see her and us. Others came too. They were very old and I was very young and I don't remember all their names. Shortly after Marjory accepted the position at New Mexico State, Grandma moved to Las Cruces to live with her. Grandma was in failing health by then and could no longer live alone. I don't know why she didn't move in with Mama and Daddy, who had been taking care of her for years. Margie had left for college by then and I soon would, so there would have been room. Marjory must have felt it was her turn.

Most of my friends went to the beach during spring break in 1976, my freshman year at Ole Miss. I had no money for a beach trip, which was just as well because Mama had other plans for me. We made another long driving trip to see Marjory, our last. Daddy couldn't get off work, so Margie's boyfriend went in his stead. The unspoken purpose of the trip was to see Grandma for the last time. She had turned 90 in January. The drive across west Texas took a full day; it was more than a hundred miles farther from Dallas to Las Cruces than from Tupelo to Dallas. After several days with Marjory and Grandma, we made the 1250-mile return trip. We had four drivers, took turns, drove all night, and arrived in Tupelo exactly 24 hours after we started.

Grandma died at home with Marjory in June the following year. She was 91, the same age as Daddy when he died 36 summers later. She was to be buried beside her husband and parents in Carlton, Texas, where she had moved with her family on the train 75 years earlier. In planning the funeral, Marjory learned that the cost of a hearse to take Grandma's remains to Carlton was prohibitive and that it was illegal to transport a body any other way. She and my cousin Andy, Aunt Elizabeth's son, decided to chance it. They rented a station wagon, folded the back seat down, and loaded the casket with help from friends. They covered it with a sheet and luggage and drove across Texas, careful not to speed. While they drove east, we drove west and met them in Carlton, where Grandma was laid to rest next to her husband. She had been a widow nearly 35 years. Dr. Brooks died 15 years before I was born and Grandma died the month before I turned 20.

Shortly after we returned from Carlton, Marjory's famous former student died unexpectedly at Graceland, his home in Memphis. Elvis and Grandma both had January birthdays and died just two months apart, but they were born 49 years apart. He was only 42. The day after his death, two of my enterprising friends went to the building where the *Tupelo Daily Journal* was printed and bought all the newspapers they could get their hands on. The headline in red declared "The King Is Dead." Then they drove to Memphis and set up shop on the sidewalk outside Graceland, where they sold the papers from the town where Elvis was born to thousands of his grieving fans. In a single day they made more than I earned for the entire summer working as a teller at Peoples Bank.

Marjory retired and moved back to Tupelo not long after Grandma died. She and Mama had been inseparable their first three decades, lived far apart the next three, and now were together again. Marjory's first house was less than a mile away from Mama and Daddy's, but that was not close enough. She found one down the street from theirs on Rogers Drive and lived there the rest of her life.

By the time they reached their mid-seventies, neither of the twins was in good health. They weren't overweight, but both smoked and neither liked to exercise. Daddy was less than eight months younger than they were chronologically, but physically he was much younger than that. He didn't smoke and hardly ever drank, worked in the yard and walked regularly, and stayed active camping with Troop 12. He never once spent a night in a hospital before he turned 80, not even when he was born. He was much healthier than Mama, who had a number of serious ailments, including breast cancer, an arterial blockage that required angioplasty, and a severe stroke when she was 74 that left her unable to speak or use her right arm. But her sharp mind was unaffected and she was able to communicate by scribbling notes left-handed and gesturing. When she was again diagnosed with cancer three years later, she made it clear that she did not want to undergo invasive treatment. Marjory's health was failing at the same time. The twins, who were born just minutes apart in the spring of 1921, died just over two months apart in the summer of 1999. I miss Marjory, but I really miss Mama.

At the visitation before Mama's funeral a friend of hers told me about a conversation between the two of them nearly 25 years earlier when Margie was a junior in college at Mama's alma mater and I was a freshman at Daddy's. She was trying to cheer Mama up about having an empty nest and told her she had enjoyed the peace and quiet when her kids left for college. She figured Mama was enjoying it too. Mama said not really, she liked it better when we were home. Her friend insisted there had to be some good things about the change. Mama thought a minute and said there was one: With Margie and me off at school, she knew when she heard a siren it couldn't be one of us. She worried about us often, but she didn't have to worry then.

Chapter 12

I can't say I know a great deal about the relationship between my parents, especially during the years after I graduated from high school and left home. They did not have much of a social life, I know that. I can't recall a single time when they went out with another couple. But if Mama was disappointed in their quiet life and modest home on Rogers Drive, I never heard her say so, and if Daddy wished things were different, he kept it to himself. And if they ever disagreed about anything, and surely they must have, they hid it from Margie and me. They got angry with us when we misbehaved, but I never once heard either of them raise a voice to the other in anger. And they didn't use profanity. I heard Daddy say "damn" once and "hell" once, but never heard Mama say either one. They were rarely affectionate in our presence other than a perfunctory kiss when Daddy left for work and again when he got home, though that was probably the times they lived in and what they learned from watching their parents. Daddy Cliff fathered four children, but it's hard for me to picture him without a necktie. There were times, though, when Daddy would overcome his upbringing, grab Mama as she walked by his chair, and pull her into his lap. I don't know if they were in love, but they were two very good people and they treated each other as good people do.

I also don't know what they truly felt about matters of religion. It seems strange to write those words because we went to church religiously, attending services at the First Methodist Church every Sunday. I believe Mama and Daddy were Bible-believing Christians, but I can't say with certainty because we didn't talk about it. We said a rote blessing every night before dinner, which we called supper, but we never prayed together otherwise and rarely mentioned faith or the Bible. But every Sunday morning Mama and Daddy would load Margie and me into the car and drive us to the church on Main Street. The four of us parted ways for Sunday school and then reunited for church. We sat together except during the years when Mama sang in the choir. Margie and I sat on either side of Daddy then. We had Sunday dinner afterwards but didn't discuss the service, the sermon, or what we believed. That was private.

For a time we went to church on Sunday evenings too. The sanctuary was darker and more beautiful at night and the music was different. There was no choir and we sang more old-time hymns, accompanied by piano instead of organ. I loved singing *come to the church in the wildwood, the little brown church in the vale, no place is so dear to my childhood as the little brown church in the vale.* Brother Bo Holloman, a happy man who loved the Boy Scouts, preached the sermons.

Long after Mama died, I found a long handwritten letter she wrote to me in December 1985. Mama had put the letter in an envelope, addressed it and put a stamp on it, but she never sent it. I guess she decided against it, but for some reason she never threw it away. She covered a range of subjects in the letter we never talked about, including religion, and wrote that she believed "the only thing in life actually worth worrying about is our relationships with other people. I am not including God in this thought because that is strictly a personal thing. How I feel about God is something to be pondered over and prayed over between me and God. It involves no one else."

After I was grown, I went camping one weekend with Daddy and my children. The kids were off playing and somehow our talk turned to religion. Daddy said he couldn't bring himself to believe that children on the other side of the world who died before they ever heard of God or Jesus weren't going to heaven. I agreed with him. It's the one and only serious conversation about religion I remember having with him. Mama was a preacher's daughter, but I can't remember ever having one with her.

Chapter 13

The world seemed to come apart in 1968. The North Vietnamese People's Army and Viet Cong launched the Tet Offensive in January. Opponents of the war in America became more strident. In April Dr. Martin Luther King was assassinated by James Earl Ray in Memphis. Sirhan Sirhan shot and killed Bobby Kennedy in Los Angeles two months later. Dr. King was only 39, Kennedy just three years older. In August fights broke out on the floor of the Democratic Convention in Chicago over the party's position on the war. Anti-war protesters rioted outside. The delegates chose status-quo candidate Hubert Humphrey over war opponent Eugene McCarthy and Mayor Daley's Chicago police violently suppressed the riots in the streets. On October 16 Tommie Smith and John Carlos, who had finished first and third in the 200-meter dash in the Mexico City Olympics with Smith breaking the world record, walked barefoot to the podium to protest poverty and then raised their gloved fists during the Star-Spangled Banner in support of black power. Twenty-two year old Bob Beamon shattered the world record in the long jump two days later, leaping more than 29 feet and breaking the old record by nearly two feet. Less than three weeks after that Richard Nixon narrowly defeated Humphrey and was chosen to be America's 37th president. Apollo 8 became the first manned spacecraft to orbit the moon on Christmas Eve, setting the stage for Neil Armstrong's giant leap for mankind the following summer.

It was an eventful year and we watched it all unfold on the black-and-white television in the new den Mama and Daddy had recently added onto the back of our home. The world was changing, but one thing did not change. Every month that year, like the 17 years before and all the years since, Troop 12 went camping. In March 1968 the troop camped for the 200th month in a row. In July I turned 11 and was finally old enough to join the troop and go with them.

For the next four years I didn't miss a single campout, though I came close in March 1971. The troop scheduled two campouts that month, one for the younger boys and an annual canoe trip on Bear Creek that was limited to Scouts 13 and older. It was the first time I was old enough for the canoe trip and I didn't want to miss it, but I had broken my arm in a sledding accident in February. I was wearing a cast and couldn't paddle, but I promised my doctor I would keep the cast dry, told Daddy it was safe because I was a good swimmer and would wear a life jacket, and convinced my friends Dan Purnell and Frank Jones to paddle me down the river. Dan may have felt guilty because he was riding on top of me on the sled when I broke my arm. I sat in the middle of the canoe, a useless passenger with a Wonder Bread plastic bag over my cast.

I became Troop 12's 125th Eagle Scout a year later, the 105th since Daddy had become the Scoutmaster a quarter century earlier. I didn't get there through favoritism. To advance in rank and earn merit badges, I had to do everything at least as well as the other boys if not better. And so I did. Not only did I love Scouts, mainly for the campouts, but I was old enough to understand that it would be a scandal if Paul Eason's son did not become an Eagle Scout. Daddy later told me he thought he would step down as Scoutmaster after my time in the troop was over. I don't know why he changed his mind, but he did, and 150 more boys became Eagles during his 20 more years as Scoutmaster and another hundred during his 15 years as an assistant.

I love to brag on Daddy and all the Eagle Scouts and all the campouts, but I tend to overlook the countless hours he spent on the mundane tasks necessary to run a Boy Scout troop. One of those tasks was planning and attending the troop's weekly meetings. On 3,000 Monday nights—50 nights a year for 60 years—Daddy put on his Scout uniform, drove to the Methodist Church, and met with the troop. He could have presided over the meetings and it would have been more efficient, but he always made it a point for the older Scouts to run them. It was part of their passage from boys to young men. His routine after the meetings didn't change much either. He drove home, dropping a few boys off along the way, then settled into his recliner with a bowl of ice cream. Without fail, he fell asleep with the TV on. A photo Mama took of him on one of those Monday nights is one of my favorites. He's in his Scout uniform, fast asleep, an empty bowl balanced in his lap. Daddy was a champion sleeper. But the trait limited what Daddy could do at night. Like me, Mama was an avid reader and loved books. She read in bed every night. Daddy tried, but he was always asleep by the second page.

Chapter 14

On October 13, 1969, Sidney Davis died in Tulsa. He was 83. As directed in his will, four trusts were established, one for his wife and one for each of his three children. The trusts were funded in part with Sidney's interests in oil and gas wells scattered across the country.

Like her daughter, Betty loved to travel. She went on an archaeological expedition to Greece and traveled to the Soviet Union when virtually nobody went there. She also took long vacations to Colorado and California. But she had little time to enjoy the income from the trust established for her benefit by her father. Betty had chronic high blood pressure and, despite repeated warnings about the risks, failed to take her medicine. A year after her father's death, when she was 58, she suffered a debilitating stroke. Her health continued to deteriorate and she died in June 1973, less than four years after Sidney's death. She was only 60.

Women live longer than men do. In the United States the difference in average life span is nearly five years. In 1947, when Betty married a man 23 older than she was, the possibility that he would outlive her was remote. But he did and by more than a decade. Herb died in the summer of 1985 at the age of 96. World War I had ended 67 years earlier. He was one of the last surviving veterans.

When Betty died, the trust for her benefit was to be divided into two separate trusts, one for Julie and one for Sid. At the time Julie was almost 35 and Sid had just turned 24. Under the terms established by their grandfather, distributions of principal were to be made to each of them on their 25th, 35th, and 40th birthdays.

Julie was already entitled to one-third of the principal in her trust and would have the right to the second third on her birthday in four months. Sid was not yet entitled to any principal distribution but would turn 25 in a year and receive one-third then.

But dividing the trust for Betty into separate trusts and making the distributions of principal on the dates directed in their grandfather's will would have been cumbersome and expensive. It would have required changing the title to multiple oil and natural gas wells in the land records of multiple states and doing so three times for Julie and three more times for Sid. Both were content for the time being to receive the income from the wells and leave all the principal in trust. They executed a revocable trust indenture in August 1973 in which they left in trust all the oil and gas properties they had inherited from their grandfather. The indenture continued the practice of quarterly income distributions and gave Julie and Sid the right to withdraw principal at any time, though they could not have withdrawn it earlier than their grandfather's will allowed.

Chapter 15

I was an enthusiastic Ole Miss football fan when I was growing up. Daddy was already grown but just as enthusiastic. Though Oxford was only 50 miles away, we went to games only occasionally—season tickets weren't in the family budget—but we listened to them on the radio every Saturday in the fall. At game time Daddy and I would pull up two chairs facing each other beside the console stereo in the living room and listen nervously as announcers Stan Torgerson and Lyman Hellums called the games. We didn't say much, but when something bad happened we'd look down and shake our heads, and when something good happened we'd look at each other and smile.

I was 12 during the 1969 season, old enough to understand football but too young to be interested in girls or know that college football players weren't gods. And Archie Manning, the Rebels' star quarterback who later played in the NFL with sons Peyton and Eli following in his footsteps, seemed like a god to me. I was impressionable and Archie was impressive.

Daddy and I weren't in the living room for the two most memorable Ole Miss games of the 1969 season. Troop 12's monthly campouts in October and November that year, just before and just after Sidney Davis died in Tulsa, happened to coincide with Ole Miss's games against Alabama and Tennessee. On the weekend of the Alabama game we camped at Tishomingo State Park northeast of Tupelo, where we built a rope bridge across Bear Creek, the same creek I would float in a canoe with a broken arm a year and a half later. Six weeks after the Tishomingo campout, the weekend of the Tennessee game, we camped and hiked at Shiloh National Military Park in Tennessee.

The Alabama game was the first ever nationally televised college football game played at night, but we didn't get to watch it. We could only listen on our portable radios as we sat by our campfires. Though Archie broke the individual single-game NCAA record for total offense with 540 yards, a record that's been broken many times in the half century since, Ole Miss lost 33–32.

The game against Tennessee six weeks later was a day game. Ole Miss was 5–3 on the season, Tennessee 7–0 and ranked third in the nation. We started our hike through the Shiloh battlefield on a beautiful autumn afternoon just as Tennessee kicked off. I was supposed to be learning about the battle and the heroics of the soldiers on both sides, but I had a radio to my ear and was focused on the game that was happening then, not the battle that was fought more than a hundred years before then. The battle was closer than the game. Ole Miss crushed the Volunteers 38–0 after losing to them 31–0 the year before.

In the locker room after the lopsided Tennessee win over the Rebels in 1968, Volunteer linebacker Steve Kiner had suggested that Archie was overrated. When asked what he thought of Archie, Kiner had responded with a question of his own: "Archie who?" After the Rebels got revenge against the Vols a year later, an Ole Miss fan got revenge against Kiner. The fan wrote a song entitled "The Ballad of Archie Who" and recorded it to the tune of Johnny Cash's "Folsom Prison Blues." It was a great time to be an Ole Miss football fan, far better than the five seasons when Daddy was in school there.

A decade later, when I was in law school and had little money to buy Christmas presents, I wrote stories for Mama and Daddy instead. The one I wrote for Daddy was about the two campouts and two Ole Miss football games in the fall of 1969, the one for Mama about my adventures in the creek beside the vacant lot where she taught me how to fish.

Chapter 16

The United States Supreme Court decided the case of *Brown v. Board of Education* in 1954 and decreed that separate schools were inherently unequal. The case returned to the court the following year, which resulted in an order requiring desegregation to proceed "with all deliberate speed." But across America and especially in the South, the next 15 years were marked by far more deliberation than speed. The process went in stages. First there was outright refusal to comply with the ruling, but the courts put a stop to that. Then came neighborhood schools, but most neighborhoods were racially segregated and so little integration was achieved. Then there was freedom of choice, which allowed parents to choose schools for their children. But few black parents chose to send their children to schools that had been all white since the day they opened and even fewer white parents chose to send their kids to predominantly black schools. As a result, until I started the eighth grade 16 years after the Supreme Court's landmark ruling, nearly all my classmates were white.

But in 1970 everything changed. Federal courts finally ran out of patience and ordered the public schools to desegregate fully and immediately. Elementary school district lines in Tupelo were redrawn to achieve racial balance, all ninth grade students were assigned to what had been the black high school named for George Washington Carver, and everyone in grades 10 through 12 was sent to Tupelo High School. Black students in the seventh and eighth grades joined us at Milam Junior High School, where Mama and Daddy had gone to school and Marjory had taught Elvis two decades earlier.

Tupelo had excellent leaders and school administrators who were committed to making desegregation work, and the city dealt with the issue far more responsibly than many in the South. Nobody stood in any of Tupelo's schoolhouse doors trying to stop black children from getting in. The city also had a smaller black population than many towns in Mississippi, which no doubt made the transition less traumatic for white parents and students in Tupelo than for those in majority-black regions. The change was probably more difficult for black students, who were suddenly far outnumbered by white classmates they had never met in new schools they had never attended.

In regions of Mississippi with large black populations, including towns in the Delta along the Mississippi River and elsewhere, white parents immediately organized private schools, so-called "seg academies," so their children could continue to attend all-white schools. No private schools were started in Tupelo and we had few problems compared to most. Some towns closed their parks and swimming pools rather than integrate them, but not Tupelo. Daddy served on the city park and recreation commission and decades later recalled that Tupelo never closed a park, a program, or a pool. Daddy liked to brag on Tupelo nearly as much as I like to brag on him.

I believe the change was probably easier for students than for their parents. The parents had all attended segregated schools. It was the natural order of things, the way it always had been and the way they believed it always should be. Desegregation was now being forced on them and there was nothing they could do. They couldn't go to school with their children to see how it was working out. Some parents were undoubtedly angry; others were worried. If Mama and Daddy were either, they didn't show it in front of Margie and me.

I also believe desegregation was less traumatic for boys than for girls. Boys of both races got to know each other before the girls did. We were thrown together on the football field in two-a-day practices even before classes started and learned quickly that the black players were not all that different from us. Some were talented and some were not, some were friendly and some were not. But we all wanted to win and, when boys or men put on uniforms, athletic or military, and pursue a common goal, color tends to fade.

All in all the transition went smoothly, at least from my perspective, but at times the cultural divide seemed wide. One day at recess two black girls got into a fight. One managed to grab the other's dress by the collar and rip it off of her. She looked down at her torn dress on the ground, then resumed the fight in her bra and panties. I stood and watched, wide-eyed. I'm sure white girls somewhere had done the same thing, but I had never witnessed anything like it. Later in the year a black classmate received his draft notice from the Army. The Vietnam War was in full swing and he was 19 and thus draft-eligible. I had no white classmates who were 19 years old.

But incidents that made us seem different were the exception, not the rule, and white and black students generally got along well, at least on the surface. Close interracial friendships were rare and interracial romances unheard of, but we were polite to our black classmates and they were polite to us. Regardless of race we were all raised in the South, and most of us had been taught to treat people with respect. I'm sure there were racial incidents, but I can't recall ever witnessing one, though perhaps that was because my focus was elsewhere. While the schools were changing, I was going through a different change, from childhood to adolescence. And like many adolescents, I was extremely self-conscious. I was less concerned about the color of my classmates than about how to talk to girls and when I was going to get body hair.

I had played quarterback on my flag football team at Joyner Elementary in the fourth grade. Most teams were coached by dads, but our coach was Jack Reed Jr., who was only in the 10th grade. He was barely old enough to drive, but I guess that made him old enough to coach. Jack loved to play football, but he didn't play for Tupelo High School that year because he still weighed less than a hundred pounds. Head coach Tom Cheney told him he needed to add some inches and pounds to keep from getting hurt when he tried out for the team. So Jack volunteered to coach us and sat in class that fall drawing up plays and defensive schemes when he was supposed to be studying.

The highlight of our season was a game we played during half-time of a Tupelo High game at Robins Field on Jefferson Street. The field, where Dr. Brooks had given the invocation before FDR's speech in 1934, was adjacent to the new Church Street School built by the WPA after the tornado destroyed the old one in 1936. The game was at night under the lights, the stands were full, and a photographer took a picture of me running around left end for a touchdown. Several years later the photo, with the word *Future* printed above it, was featured in the program handed out to those who attended the high school's games. Whoever was in charge of the program should have picked someone else. In the years after the fourth grade many boys passed me by in size and speed and, by the time I reached the eighth grade, I couldn't compete. I was the past, not the future. Jack's football future was brighter than mine. He grew enough to play, caught a touchdown pass his senior season, and thought it would be the happiest moment of his life when the band struck up the school fight song while he was lying in the end zone holding the ball.

I played one last year in the ninth grade at Carver before I faced reality and gave it up. Anybody could be on the football team at Carver and most ninth-grade boys chose to join. It was the thing to do and we did it. We had a huge squad with many benchwarmers who rarely got to play. I was one of them. As we stood on the sidelines and watched our team win game after game, we needed an outlet for our energy. Midway through the season one of us got excited after we scored a touchdown and celebrated by throwing his helmet straight up and catching it when it came down. When we scored again, the rest of us copied him. Because we were 14-year-old boys, the celebrations turned into competitions to see who could throw his helmet the highest and still catch it.

Going into our next to last game, we still had a perfect record. The game was at Corinth, 50 miles north of Tupelo on the Tennessee state line, and was the second game in a home-and-away season series. We had played them in Tupelo early in the season and won easily, but the rematch was different. Late in the fourth quarter the score was tied at eight, but we were driving. Quarterback Mark Murphy threw a long pass down the middle to our fastest receiver, Scotty Lambert. He didn't catch it, but there was obvious pass interference and one of the referees threw a flag. A penalty wouldn't ordinarily have been cause for celebration, but through three quarters there had been little to cheer so helmets, including mine, were launched.

As mine reached its peak and started its descent, I saw an object coming toward me out of the corner of my eye. The object was assistant coach Travis Beard. He was walking fast, his eyes on the field, not on my helmet. I reached up to try to grab it, but he was nearly a foot taller than I was and I couldn't get to it. It hit him squarely on top of the head, sounding like a rifle shot. He dropped to his knees and my helmet rolled onto the field. After a few seconds that seemed like many more, he shook his head, slowly got to his feet, and retrieved the helmet. He then turned to face the bench. In the Bible Belt in 1971 coaches didn't use profanity, at least not in my experience, but when Coach Beard asked whose helmet it was he added a modifier.

The answer was obvious because I was the only one still standing there. My teammates who'd been beside me had all slunk away. I confessed and apologized and he thrust the helmet into my chest and ordered me to keep it on my head. I had already decided to do that. We didn't score and the game ended in a tie. It was a long bus ride home—longest of all for me. The next morning before class I returned my uniform to the gym. Head coach Mickey Linder, a fine coach and finer man, grinned when he saw me. He said he'd wondered the night before if he would now be our only coach when he heard the crack of helmet on skull and saw Coach Beard down on his knees. We won our last game easily and scored 36 points, but I didn't throw my helmet. None of my teammates did either.

Forty years after the game against Corinth, almost to the day, Carrie and I took Daddy back to Tupelo on November 4, 2011, two months after he moved in with us. It was his 90th birthday. Carrie, the thoughtful one in our marriage, had organized a party for him in the fellowship hall at First Methodist Church. Before the party we went to the lunch meeting of the Kiwanis Club, which Daddy had attended for more than five decades. Jack Reed Jr., who had been elected mayor of Tupelo two years earlier, gave a short speech and presented Daddy with the key to the city. It had been 45 years since Jack coached my flag football team and 46 since he became one of Daddy's Eagle Scouts. I saw Coach Beard at the meeting and spoke to him about the night in Corinth and apologized again. He had forgiven, but he had not forgotten. After the birthday party that afternoon we gathered around a computer screen and watched the video that had been made that morning of Congressman Alan Nunnelee as he presented a resolution on the floor of the House of Representatives honoring Daddy for his lifetime of service to Tupelo and the boys of Troop 12. When I asked Daddy that night if he'd had a good birthday, he said he couldn't wait till next year.

In the 10th grade I changed schools and sports—from Carver to Tupelo High and from football to tennis. Puddie Ruff, my aunt, was our coach. I was better at tennis than at football and played mixed doubles my sophomore year and boys' doubles as a junior and senior. Jack's brother Scott and I made it to the semifinals of the state tournament my senior year, but I played poorly and we lost in straight sets. My modest high school athletic career was over.

Not long after graduation I played in a mixed doubles tournament with my cousin Missy, Puddie's daughter. We won three close matches and made it to the final, which was the closest of all. The third and final set went to a nine-point tiebreaker. After six points we were tied and I was scheduled to serve the last three. I was serving well and we won the first point easily. We now needed just one more point, but I promptly double-faulted for the first time all day. That made it match point for both teams. Whoever won the next point would win the game, set, match, and tournament. My first serve was long, which left me with a dilemma. I had just missed three serves in a row. Back-to-back double faults to lose the tournament would be horrifying. There were two dozen spectators in the stands beside the court. Even they would be embarrassed. I was tempted to play it safe and lob it in, but that would be shameful even if we won. I served at normal speed, the ball somehow went in, we won the point, and I was able to breathe again.

I was also better at tennis than at girls. The prospect of kissing one made me more nervous than missing three serves in a row in the tiebreaker. I was a late bloomer and didn't have a girlfriend until my senior year, when I began dating Susan Eskridge, a sophomore. On New Year's Eve we were invited to a party at a friend's house and I picked her up in Mama's Ford LTD. I decided to take a shortcut on a dirt road, but it had been raining and we got stuck in the mud. We walked back to Susan's house, called our friends to explain our whereabouts, and then called Daddy, who picked us up in the big Troop 12 van we called the White Elephant. We returned to the site where we'd left the LTD in the mud so he could pull it out, but it was gone. We feared it had been stolen, but our friends confessed that they had gotten there first, hooked it up to a Ford Bronco, and towed it to a secluded spot out in the country near the site of the party. Susan and I made it to the car just before midnight and never made it to the party.

Susan was my first true love and we had wonderful times together, but the relationship didn't survive my leaving for college the following year. Nearly 35 years later she and I were both divorced and both living in Jackson and we went out two or three times. I pointed out that we had last dated two-thirds of our lives ago and she asked how I had changed. I told her I thought the biggest difference was that I was now much less self-conscious, which said more about me at 17 when I was scared of girls than about me at 51. We had a good time and I thought we might wind up getting back together, but we were both going out with other people and the opportunity passed.

Chapter 17

Julie relapsed after her first stint in rehab. Much had happened in her life in recent years that made a permanent recovery difficult. She had moved from Denver to Salt Lake City, then to Colombia, then back to Tulsa. Her marriage had ended and her grandfather had died, as had both of her parents. Not long after Betty's death, Julie was admitted to rehab again. Sid made her go, as he did over and over. There she met a handsome young man from Michigan, Mark Hutchison, who was nearly 15 years younger than she was. They began dating, got married, and moved to Colorado, where Julie bought a home for them in Snowmass. To pay for it, she made one phone call to Lewis Bettman in St. Louis. She asked him to handle the transaction but did not say how. He made the necessary arrangements. She later traded up to a beautiful home on the Roaring Fork River in Aspen. Cher, who was recently divorced from Sonny, lived down the road.

While Julie and Mark were living in Aspen, she decided she needed a will. It was August of 1978, three months before her 40th birthday. The will left all her jewelry, with two exceptions, to her stepsister Sandy, who by then was married to Joe Buell and had three teenage sons. The exceptions were her wedding ring, which she left to Mark, and her grandmother's diamond watch, which she left to Sid's daughter Libby. She left everything else in trust to Mark if they were still married and to Sandy's three sons if they weren't. The terms of the will highlighted the difference in age between Julie and Mark. Half the principal of the trust for his benefit would be distributed to him when he turned 30 and the other half when he turned 40. Julie named Lewis Bettman as both executor of her estate and trustee of the trust to be established when she died.

Chapter 18

Daddy was a Southern gentleman with impeccable manners. He stood whenever a woman entered the room, opened doors for everyone, and took off his hat when he came inside. He never told me to do any of those things, but he didn't have to. I watched and copied him. Hundreds of other boys copied him as well. Daddy was also self-reliant. He was handy around the house and mowed his big yard with a push mower until he was in his mid-eighties. He never suggested that I mow my own yard, but I do. Daddy was an exceptional leader as well, but he led by example, not by giving orders. He was more of a doer than a talker and rarely gave advice except when asked. And because I didn't ask, I don't remember ever talking to him about where I should go to college, what I should study, or what I should be when I grew up. He probably figured I would ask if I wanted his opinion, but like most teenagers I thought I had it all figured out.

I graduated from high school in May 1975 and decided after little deliberation to go to college at Ole Miss. I briefly considered other schools, including Millsaps College in Jackson, where I might have been able to play on the tennis team, but I had been planning to go to Ole Miss for as long as I could remember. Changing course would have taken something dramatic and nothing dramatic happened.

I've now been a lawyer more than 35 years. I suppose it suits me, though being a lawyer is the only permanent job I've ever had so it's impossible to know if anything else would have suited me better. But I didn't seriously consider anything else. Law and medicine were the most obvious choices for good students in Mississippi in the 1970s, but I had little to go by in picking between the two. There were no lawyers in my family and I didn't know any. I had no idea what lawyers did other than what I'd seen on TV, which I learned when I became a real lawyer was far from realistic. But I knew a few things. I knew I liked English and history more than science and math, and I knew I didn't want to be a doctor. So I chose political science when I was asked to pick a major. It sounded interesting, though I gave no thought to what I could do with a political science degree if I decided not to go to law school or didn't get in.

I was excited when the time came to leave for college, but I was also apprehensive because I had never been away from home or Mama and Daddy for more than a week or two. I had few belongings and no car, so Daddy drove me the 50 miles to Oxford. Along the way he did something uncharacteristic. He had been a member and president of Phi Delta Theta fraternity during his years at Ole Miss and I was about to go through fraternity rush. As we neared Oxford, he said he wanted me to join the fraternity I preferred. That didn't surprise me. But then he added something that did. If it was a close call, he said, it would mean a lot to him for us to be fraternity brothers. It was a close call before then but not after. I joined Phi Delta Theta and had a wonderful time in Oxford. I made good grades and still had an abundance of free time. It was the four most carefree years of my life. Ole Miss also had a better record against Mississippi State when I was in school than when Daddy was. We won two and lost two.

During the summers when I was at Ole Miss, I returned to Tupelo, lived at home, and worked at Peoples Bank. Going to summer school in Oxford would have been much more fun, but I needed to live rent-free and earn spending money. Also, unlike when Daddy was at Ole Miss, there wasn't a war looming and I had no reason to graduate early. I worked as a teller for three summers and an auditor the summer between undergrad and law school.

A number of my high school friends also came home from college each summer. One of them had access to his parents' ski boat.

After work one Friday a group of us drove to Pickwick Lake on the Tennessee River, launched the boat, and camped on a sandbar. After skiing the next morning, we pulled into a cove where a dozen other boats were already anchored. At the head of the cove was a waterfall 30 feet high. Over the years thousands of visitors have climbed to the top and jumped, landing in the deep water below. The waterfall is usually not dangerous, but beer and testosterone made it dangerous that day.

After we had been in the cove for two hours, four beers, and six jumps off the fall, jumping was no longer good enough. To make things more exciting and try to impress the girls in the other boats, some of us dove off the top, others did flips, and one climbed a tree at the top to add 10 feet to the jump. Next a group of us lined up across the top and jumped simultaneously. Then my friend Marion Winkler suggested I climb onto his back. He would jump and we would ride down together.

I agreed because I would have agreed to anything, though I also figured I was safe because I would be on top. But I was wrong. When Marion hit the water, his head snapped back, hit my chin, and knocked me out. I sank below the surface. By the time I bobbed to the top nearly a minute later, people were diving off their boats trying to find me. I waved off their help, swam back to our boat, climbed in, and opened another beer. Though I talked to my buddies for the next half hour, I remembered none of it later. Then, suddenly, I came to my senses.

Chapter 19

In August 1978, the same month Julie signed her will in Aspen and just before my senior year at Ole Miss, I took the Law School Admission Test and began the process of applying to law schools. After the Christmas break I got engaged to Betsy Ann Simpson. We had met on a blind date in the spring of my freshman year when she was a senior in high school. While she planned the wedding, I narrowed my law school choices to Duke and the Universities of Texas and Virginia. I had never visited any of them and had neither the time nor the money to do so. Cost was also a key factor in choosing a school. Texas and UVA were public universities with much lower tuition than at Duke, a private school. But Duke offered me a scholarship and Betsy Ann a job in the law library and Texas and UVA gave me no financial aid. We made plans to move to North Carolina after we got married.

Our wedding was the second Saturday in May, less than a week after I took my last exam. I missed my graduation ceremony so we could leave on our honeymoon on my very first flight. We lived with Mama and Daddy that summer and I worked as an auditor at the bank and Betsy Ann as a day camp counselor at city park. In August we loaded a U-Haul with old furniture I'd refinished at nights and on weekends and headed east. I drove the U-Haul accompanied by our dog Josey, named for Clint Eastwood's character in *The Outlaw Josey Wales*. Betsy Ann followed in my first car, a used red Datsun 200SX Mama and Daddy had given me as a combination graduation/wedding present. Her mother Ann rode with her. Like Mama, Ann was an identical twin. She and Betsy were 10 years younger than Mama and Marjory, but their birthdays were only a day apart. Mama and Marjory were born on March 16, 1921, Ann and Betsy on March 15, 1931. They were sweet and fun and I loved both of them. They had eight children between them. Betsy Ann was the only girl and was named for both of them.

We made it to Asheville, North Carolina, the first day and the next morning Betsy Ann and Ann decided to tour Biltmore, the magnificent mansion built by George Washington Vanderbilt in the late 1800s. I was ready to get to our apartment and start unpacking so I skipped Biltmore and continued east to Durham with Josey.

That summer I had lost my wedding band while playing golf. I had worn it less than a month. I searched the course, retracing my route on each hole, but couldn't find it. We needed furniture more than I needed a new ring so I was still without one when I pulled into Chapel Tower Apartments in Durham at noon. Josey had been riding with me in the cab all morning and, when I opened the door, she immediately raced around to the back of the nearest building. By the time I caught up with her, she had befriended a sunbathing coed. I introduced myself and Josey and said we'd just arrived and were moving in. She asked which apartment. I gave her the number and she said she lived in the same building. I returned to the U-Haul, unloaded what I could by myself, then left with Josey to see about getting the utilities turned on.

While I was gone, two things happened: The girl stuck a note in our apartment door inviting Josey and me to dinner and Betsy Ann arrived and found the note. With her telling me what to write, I responded with a note to the girl declining the invitation but adding that my wife and I looked forward to getting to know her. Forty years earlier Daddy had scraped together $25 to buy a Model T Ford. The next week Betsy Ann and I came up with enough money to buy me a new wedding band.

I had three good years at Duke and became lifelong friends with great people from all over the country, though I had to study much harder and had much less free time than at Ole Miss. I worked for law firms in Memphis the summer after my first year and Atlanta the summer after my second. I enjoyed my time with both and planned to join a firm eventually, but I didn't accept a permanent job starting right after I finished school. Instead, because Betsy Ann and I were thinking we might want to return to Mississippi, I applied for a clerkship in Jackson with Charles Clark, the Chief Judge of the United States Court of Appeals for the Fifth Circuit. The clerkship would be for my first year after graduation and give us more time to decide where we wanted to live.

Judge Clark could have played a judge in the movies if he hadn't been one. He was tall and handsome and had perfect white hair. He had gravitas. I came to Jackson for him to interview me during the summer when I was working in Atlanta. Near the end of our discussion he said something I wasn't expecting. He told me he believed judges should choose clerks rather than vice versa. For that reason his practice was to consider only those applicants who had expressed a commitment to work for him if he decided to select them. He thus wanted to know if I wanted the job. Before the interview Betsy Ann and I had not yet decided if we wanted to come to Jackson for my first year after law school. I figured we could decide later if I got an offer. And I'm certain the judge would have understood if I had said I needed to talk to my wife before letting him know. But as I sat before the Chief Judge in his chambers, that didn't seem like the thing to say. All I could manage was "sure, your honor." He said he was interviewing another applicant immediately and would be making a decision very soon.

I left the courthouse and walked across Capitol Street for another interview, this one with a large Jackson law firm. Two hours later Judge Clark called the firm, they tracked me down in a partner's office and put me on the line, and the judge notified me that I would be clerking for him. He said his staff would be in touch with details. The conversation lasted less than two minutes. That evening Betsy Ann was surprised to learn we would be moving to Jackson but pleased we would be closer to her friends and family, especially her mother. Judge Clark was a wonderful man and a great judge and the year I spent working for him was a rewarding experience. Both then and later, lawyers would ask me if they wanted Judge Clark to be assigned to appeals they were handling. My answer was always the same: "You want him if it's a case you should win but not if it's a case you should lose because he's going to get it right."

I never had nice dress shoes when I was growing up. I usually wore penny loafers and would get them half a size too small because they were cheap and they stretched. Before I started at Ole Miss, Daddy decided it was time for me to have some real dress shoes. One Saturday morning we drove to the Progressive Shoe Store in Pontotoc, a small town between Tupelo and Oxford. We settled on a pair of black Allen Edmonds wingtips, by far the nicest and most expensive shoes I'd ever owned. They were excellent shoes, but I made a mistake in selecting the size. Consistent with past practice, I bought them half a size too small. But unlike past practice, they didn't stretch. And they hurt my feet.

For the next seven years, as I moved to Oxford, then to Durham, then to Jackson, the too-small shoes moved with me, going from closet to closet and gathering dust. Once every year or so, choosing hope over experience, I would wipe off the dust and wear them. I don't know if I thought they would get bigger or my feet would get smaller, but neither happened. They still hurt my feet.

One of those hopeful days was while I was working for Judge Clark. Walter Weems and Bob Morrison from the Brunini firm in Jackson, which was recruiting me, called that morning and asked me to lunch. We met at the Elite, a famous Jackson restaurant two blocks down Capitol Street from the courthouse. After lunch, as the three of us started back up the sidewalk, Walter noticed that I was wincing with each step and walking with a slight limp. He asked if I had sprained my ankle. I said no, confessed that my shoes were too small, and told them about the foolish purchase years earlier. The shoes were old, I said, but they were practically brand new. As we continued, I noticed that Bob was looking down at my feet. After a few more steps, he offered an assessment of his own shoes. "You know what," he said, "my shoes are a little too big." We then did the obvious. We sat down on the steps of the building we were passing and swapped shoes. The relief was immediate. His fit me; mine fit him. Both of our problems were solved.

The second-hand shoes I got that day became my wedding,

funeral, and courtroom shoes for the next decade. By the time they finally wore out after being resoled three times, Bob had left the law practice to join his family business in Vicksburg, 50 miles west of Jackson. I boxed up the shoes, mailed them back to him, and included a note thanking him for letting me borrow them.

We decided to stay in Jackson after my year with the judge and I joined the Brunini firm, where I spent the next 22 years. Betsy Ann and I had three children born three years apart: Ann Lowrey, named for Betsy Ann's mother, was born in 1984; Cliff, named for Daddy Cliff, in 1987; and Paul, named for Daddy, in 1990. My sister Margie's three children were born the same years ours were. Her husband Brendan grew up in Scotland and speaks with a wonderful Scottish brogue. Their relationship began while both were working aboard a Carnival cruise ship. She worked in a gift shop; he was in pest control. When they got married, they took jobs with the company ashore. Margie gave up her job after they had children, but Brendan stayed with the company and rose through the ranks of management. He ultimately became senior vice president of marine operations, a position in which he oversaw the entire fleet of Carnival ships. They live in Davie, a suburb of Fort Lauderdale, and he's now retired and plays golf at Grande Oaks Golf Club, where *Caddyshack* was filmed.

I took my children camping when they were young and returned occasionally to Tupelo to camp with Daddy and the Scouts. In March 1993 I did both. When Daddy and Troop 12 camped for the 500th consecutive month, Ann Lowrey, Cliff, and I camped with them. We met them at Camp Yocona, the Boy Scout camp west of Tupelo where I spent a week each summer when I was in the troop. Betsy Ann did not like to camp and Paul was too young, but they came with Mama to the banquet in the dining hall on Saturday night. Daddy had just stepped down as head Scoutmaster and former members of Troop 12 living all over America returned for the celebration in part to see old friends but also to honor him. After the campout I wrote him a letter and told him he was my hero.

To thank Daddy for his many years of service to the troop, the men who had become Eagle Scouts under his leadership made contributions for a special gift. The assistant Scoutmaster in charge of the festivities suggested commissioning a bronze bust of Daddy to be placed outside the troop's headquarters. I objected because I knew Daddy would not want anything so grand. He would be honored but embarrassed. He was not a bust kind of guy.

The donations were instead used to pay for two trips. The Scouts gave Mama and Daddy a wonderful tour of California they never would have taken on their own and gave Daddy a raft trip on the Middle Fork of the Salmon River in Idaho. Those who wanted to join him could go on their own nickel. I was among the 35 former Troop 12 members and their children who joined Daddy on the Middle Fork in July 1994. I took Ann Lowrey, who had just turned 10. She was the youngest person and the only girl on what proved to be a magnificent trip. We saw wildlife every day, caught cutthroat trout on dry flies in the crystal clear water, and hiked up a creek to a hot spring that had been dammed to form a hot tub by Chinese miners a century earlier. After the Middle Fork it was hard to persuade Ann Lowrey to camp in Mississippi.

Chapter 20

Julie's second marriage, like her first, did not last. Her drinking again led to problems. Mark tried to get her to stop, or at least cut back, and he called Julie's former roommate Brenda Boone, who was now Brenda Davis, to ask for her help. Brenda and her husband Bob tried, as did Sid Smith and Lewis Bettman. And Julie tried too, but never for long.

In early 1980 Lewis got a call from Mark asking if he would mediate the terms of their divorce. Lewis said he would do so but only if Julie agreed. She joined in the request and they soon reached an agreement. Mark took a few things, including their boat, and returned to his native Michigan. Julie kept the rest. She had already sold the beautiful home on the Roaring Fork in Aspen and moved back to Tulsa. The divorce was finalized on May 1, 1980. The end of Julie's second marriage came 10 years after the end of her first.

Julie was now 41, twice divorced, both her parents were gone, and she lived alone. But she still had good times. She still enjoyed travel and loved to find just the right gifts to bring home to her friends. She bought a bottle of violet liqueur for Lewis in Paris, which he used to season his coffee. She treated Sandy Buell to a magnificent trip to Africa, including a photo safari and a tour of the pyramids and the Sphinx. Sandy, who was a gifted artist and photographer, was grateful to Julie for her generosity and the two had a wonderful time together. And when Julie was home in Tulsa, she enjoyed spending time with Sid and his family. On summer afternoons he would take Sid Jr. and Libby to swim in the pool at

Julie's home on 48th Street. She loved the children and had fun when they came to see her.

But then they went home and Julie was alone. And with no job, no husband, and no children, she had too much time on her hands, which meant too much time to drink. She would begin the day with a vodka and grapefruit juice and go from there. Julie would have benefited from having to earn a living, having to get up in the morning, get dressed, and go to work. Wealthy families are often too generous to their children. The desire to provide security for them is understandable, but giving them so much that they don't have to work does them no favors. Warren Buffett, one of the world's richest men, said he wanted to give his children enough so they could do anything but not so much that they could do nothing. In all likelihood Julie would have been better off personally if she had been worse off financially.

One afternoon several years after her return from Aspen, Sid got a call from one of Julie's neighbors who had spotted her lying unconscious on the floor of her home. An ambulance was called and she was rushed to the hospital, where she regained consciousness. The staff did a full assessment. Julie was not injured from the fall, but her liver was found to be severely diseased. Her doctor studied the test results and gave her an ultimatum: quit or die.

Not long after that incident, Julie called Lewis Bettman and offered him a gift, her 12-cylinder Jaguar, "the twelve" as she called it. It was a beautiful car but always seemed to be in the shop. He thought she was joking, but she insisted she wasn't. She told him to come get it and he flew to Tulsa to drive it home to St. Louis.

When Lewis arrived, Julie was as kind and gracious as always, but she was in bad shape. It was obvious she was drinking heavily. Lewis opened her refrigerator and found only two items inside, a bottle of vodka for Julie and a can of food for her cat. The situation appeared hopeless. The Jaguar seemed almost like a parting gift.

On Sunday, April 13, 1986, I watched on CBS as Jack Nicklaus shot a 65 at Augusta National to win the Masters and become the oldest champion in the tournament's history, a title he still holds. He was 46. The next day, in St. John Medical Center in Tulsa, Julie died. She was 47. She had again been found unconscious, but this time she did not recover. She had been told she would die if she did not quit drinking. She did not quit, and so she died. The coroner determined that the cause of death was cirrhosis of the liver. It was a sad end to a short life that had held such promise. She had gone from being the girl who had everything to drowning in the bottle. Like her mother before her, she was married twice, divorced twice, and died much too young.

Though she did not have a job for the last two decades of her life, Julie still died a millionaire. She owned a significant portfolio of stocks and bonds as well as interests in numerous oil and gas wells. Initially it appeared that she had no last will and testament directing what to do with it all. Lewis wondered if she had signed a will somewhere along the way, tracked down Mark Hutchison in Michigan, and asked if he knew of anything. Mark revealed that Julie had signed a will when they were living in Aspen and gave Lewis the name of the lawyer who drafted it. Lewis obtained the will and submitted it to the probate court in Tulsa.

Because Mark and Julie were divorced, he was no longer a beneficiary of her will. The bulk of her estate was to be placed in trust for the benefit of Sandy's three sons. In 1989, three years after Julie's death, Sid and Sandy reached an agreement in which all of Julie's stocks and bonds were placed in the trust for the Buell brothers and Sid and his family acquired Julie's oil and gas interests.

Lee Farnham was living in Seattle when Julie died. They had been divorced more than 15 years and nobody thought to tell him the news. Near the end of 1986, as was his custom, Lee mailed Julie a card wishing her a Merry Christmas. He expected her to respond, as was her custom, but she did not. Weeks later he received a note from Sandy informing him that Julie had died.

Chapter 21

Three months after Julie died, I nearly did. Like Julie, I had a Volkswagen. Mine was a '68 Beetle we had bought for a few hundred dollars from Betsy Ann's great-aunt, a professor and actress and wonderful woman from Memphis named Betty May Collins. The Beetle had no air-conditioning and was so old the seat belts didn't work. I was driving home from work on a hot July afternoon a week after my 29th birthday when I topped a hill on West Street and a car pulled out in front of me. I swerved to miss it and hit another car coming from the opposite direction head-on. An ambulance was called but couldn't take me to the hospital right away. The damage to the Beetle was so extensive that jaws of life had to be brought to the scene to get me out. Fortunately the driver of the other car, which was newer and more substantial than the Beetle, was unhurt. As at Pickwick Lake a decade earlier, I have no memory of what happened next, but my actions were soon reported to Frank Quiriconi, the CEO of the hospital where I was treated. The next day, after I regained my senses, they were reported to me.

The ambulance driver first drove me to the University of Mississippi Medical Center, a teaching hospital near the site of the wreck, but I refused to let them take me inside. Instead I demanded to be taken to St. Dominic's Hospital, which the Brunini firm represented and for which I had done legal work. The ambulance driver complied and drove me to St. Dominic's, where I was wheeled into the emergency room. I had symptoms of a head injury so the nurse gave me a neurological exam, asking me a series of questions—my name, date of birth, address, and the like. I answered them all correctly, or so I was told, until she asked me who the president was. I was supposed to say Ronald Reagan, but instead I said Frank Quiriconi.

Word of my answer to the question as well as my demand to come to his hospital reached Frank quickly, and he called and came to see me the next day. I had a brain hemorrhage and a cracked kneecap, which was a steep price to pay for a chance to demonstrate my loyalty to a good client, but I soon recovered from both. All I had left was an excuse. For years I blamed the hemorrhage when I couldn't remember someone's name. I've always been good with dates and numbers but terrible with names.

Four months after my wreck Daddy turned 65 and retired from his last job in the private sector, as a human resources manager at a plant north of Tupelo that made heavy equipment. But he didn't stay unemployed for long. Friends asked him to run for the Tupelo City Council, to follow in Daddy Cliff's footsteps. Daddy was reluctant—he was neither the political type nor a gregarious glad-hander—but he never turned down a request to help others, especially if it meant helping Tupelo. Daddy loved Tupelo. Other than four years at Ole Miss, three in the Navy, and two with Carrie and me at the end of his life, he spent all of his more than nine decades there. So he agreed to run for the city-wide at-large Council seat. Though campaigning was foreign to him, people knew what kind of man he was and he won easily. He was reelected to two more four-year terms before deciding not to seek a fourth term when he was almost 80. Daddy never hung on to anything too long, be it Scoutmaster or the City Council or anything else. When he realized it was time to quit driving, he gave his old minivan to one of his grandsons and never drove again.

During his time on the City Council Daddy's fellow members chose him to serve as vice mayor and he became the acting mayor when the incumbent resigned to take a position with the TVA. Not long after Mama died, Daddy took a trip to Scotland with a group from the First Methodist Church, a rare occasion on which he spent money on himself. Mike Armour, who was on the trip, introduced Daddy to the locals as the mayor of Tupelo. Mike told me later that Daddy got a great deal of attention from Scottish women who wanted to have their pictures taken with the handsome mayor and that he didn't seem to mind at all.

Chapter 22

When Ann Lowrey, Cliff, and Paul were young, they often went to Tupelo to spend weekends with Mama and Daddy, who were always willing to give us a break and enjoyed spending time with their grandchildren. Sometimes one or two of the children would go but sometimes all three. In the early '90s we needed a large vehicle for carpool and family trips and got Betsy Ann a black Suburban, which we used to deliver the children. One of us would take them on Friday afternoon or Saturday morning and retrieve them on Sunday afternoon. Our rendezvous point was the McDonald's in Kosciusko, a small town in central Mississippi named for the Polish general who fought for the patriots in the Revolutionary War. The kids thought the name of the McDonald's was Kosciusko's. To get there we drove north on the Natchez Trace and Mama and Daddy drove south. Their drive was 30 miles longer than ours, but that's the way they wanted it.

Cypress Swamp, an oxbow lake that was left behind when the Pearl River cut through a curve and rerouted itself long ago, runs along the east side of the Trace north of Jackson. The swamp is filled with cypresses and Tupelo gums, among the few trees that can survive for long periods in standing water. Cliff, Paul, and I got an early start one Saturday morning when I was taking them to meet Mama and Daddy so we could stop on our way at Cypress Swamp. Walking along the trail, we spotted a small alligator four or five feet long lying on top of the water. We yelled and splashed trying to get it to move, but the alligator ignored us. We continued to Kosciusko, where I delivered the boys to Mama and Daddy, and they returned to Tupelo.

Late the next afternoon I drove up to Kosciusko again. When I pulled into McDonald's, Cliff bounded out of Daddy's minivan and came charging across the parking lot. He demanded vindication. "Tell him, Daddy. Tell Big Paul we saw an alligator at Cypress Swamp. He doesn't believe me. Tell him." Daddy had appeared by now and was standing behind Cliff smiling. I confirmed that Cliff was indeed telling the truth, that we had seen an alligator at Cypress Swamp. Cliff looked pleased until Daddy asked a question based on Cliff's description of the alligator: "Was it as big as the Suburban?" Cliff's expression shifted from satisfied to sheepish.

Chapter 23

Mama was an artist. Many of her paintings and drawings hang on the walls of our home in Ridgeland and I have two in my office. Her paintings of ducks, two of my favorites, hung over the bed in Mama and Daddy's bedroom for more than 50 years. Carrie and I had them reframed and now they're in our bedroom.

When we cleaned out the house Mama and Daddy had lived in since the year before I was born, we found a number of treasures: Daddy's flight log from after the war recording a flight on November 20, 1946, the day he was shot at over the Mississippi State campus; documents from his early years as the Scoutmaster of Troop 12, including a list of contributions and expenses that balanced to the penny for the construction of a new building for the troop; and a scrapbook Mama and Marjory kept that was filled with love notes from boys and newspaper articles from their time at MSCW, which Marjory referred to decades later as Mississippi's Sweetest Collection of Women.

In the top drawer of Daddy's dresser I discovered another treasure, a copy of an old issue of *Sports Illustrated* with the cover missing. It was dated November 15, 1954. Daddy started subscribing to the magazine in the late '60s when I was an avid St. Louis Cardinals baseball fan and Ole Miss/Archie Manning football fan, but we didn't get it before then. So where did Mama and Daddy get the single issue from 1954, three years before I was born and two years before they moved into the home on Rogers Drive? And why did they keep it? I went through it from front to back looking for the answers.

Reading the magazine was like going back in time. On the second page was an article entitled "How to Be a Cheerleader," which noted that head cheerleader Laura Paul at Warren Harding High in Bridgeport, Connecticut, paid for her uniform by working at the notions counter at Woolworth's. Pages four and five contained a list of all major universities in America with enrollment and stadium capacity. I was struck by how few women went to college in the middle of the last century. In 1954 Ole Miss had 2,600 students, only 800 of whom were women. The ratio at Mississippi State was even more lopsided, with only 300 coeds among the 2,700 in school there. Now both schools have an enrollment of more than 20,000 and more women than men go to college in America. In 1954 both Alabama and Auburn had more students than Ole Miss and Mississippi State but smaller stadiums. Bear Bryant didn't become the coach in Tuscaloosa for four more years. On page 62 was an article about perennial football loser Slippery Rock, which at the time had 830 students and now has nearly 10 times that many. The article included a photo of two couples slow dancing with this caption: "Informal Dance Night Before Game Followed Pep Rally. Dance Was Over By 11."

Sports Illustrated was a brand new magazine in November 1954. The very first issue was published only three months before then. In its early years *SI* covered hunting and fishing in addition to the sports it covers today. On page 40 of the November 15 issue was an article by Florence Stumpf entitled "The Ducks Are Flying South Again." Stumpf, co-author of the definitive book *Sports in American Life*, began her article with this sentence: "The chill north winds are sweeping across the plains and prairies of Canada, the breeding and nesting grounds of North American ducks, and the great southward migrations have begun." So it was in November 1954 and so it still is every November.

Stumpf's article was accompanied by paintings of 16 different species of ducks by artist Athos Menaboni. Among the paintings I found the answer to why this issue of *Sports Illustrated* was still in a drawer in the house on Rogers Drive nearly 60 years after it was published. Two of Menaboni's ducks, the Shoveller and

Ruddy Duck, served as the models for Mama's ducks that now hang in our bedroom. I thought initially that Mama had painted the mirror image of Menaboni's Shoveller because his duck faces right and hers left, but with an internet search I found a left-facing Shoveller on the cover of the magazine, the cover that's missing from the issue I found in Tupelo. The Shoveller on the cover and Mama's Shoveller are identical. Mama would never have claimed she was an accomplished original artist, but she was very good at painting what she saw.

I never spoke to Mama about the magazine because I never saw it while she was alive, but she must have seen it on a newsstand, admired the duck on the cover, and bought it. She then used that duck and another one she found in the middle as models for the ducks she painted, and she kept the two paintings and the magazine for the rest of her life. Now I have all three.

Chapter 24

Before Ann Lowrey was old enough to babysit for her brothers, we had three consecutive babysitters who were the children of our friends Jerry and Kathy Drake. Ruthie was the oldest and babysat until she left for college, when Brian replaced her. When he graduated from high school, Jonny took over.

In the spring of 1994, near the end of Jonny's junior year at Jackson Preparatory School, his parents decided to leave Jackson. Jerry was a petroleum geologist and the oil and gas business in Mississippi was in a deep recession. They moved to Columbia Falls, Montana, where Kathy's brother lived. Jonny understood why his parents needed to move but wasn't thrilled about moving with them. He was a star on the Jackson Prep soccer team, had a beautiful girlfriend and, like Mama and Marjory when their parents moved to Greenwood in 1938, didn't want to leave his friends and go to a new school in a new city for his senior year. He was also seeking an appointment to a military academy, which requires support from a member of Congress. Jonny had secured that support in Mississippi but only if he was in school here. He would be starting from scratch in Montana. We decided to invite him to spend the year with us.

Friends gave us credit for taking Jonny in, but we had a wonderful year with him, probably our best ever. Betsy Ann and I and all three of our children loved Jonny then and still do. He was far more mature and considerate at 17 than I was. He was always willing to babysit and help around the house and he and I enjoyed epic battles on our miniature ping pong table. The only downside to having Jonny live with us was the effect on our grocery bill. He seemed to eat as much as the other five of us combined. At dinner I sat at one end of the table, he sat at the other, and at the end of the meal the rest of us passed our plates to him so he could eat what was left.

But the grocery bill was far exceeded in value by Jonny's company and friendship, and we hated to see him go when the school year ended. After Jonny graduated in May 1995, we were joined at the Jackson Amtrak station by his crying girlfriend to see him off on the long train trip to the Drakes' new home in Montana. From there he went to West Point, where he excelled on the soccer field and in the classroom. He spent every Thanksgiving with us and came to Jackson on other occasions with his classmates and teammates. It was clear that they loved him too. In May 1999 Betsy Ann, the children, and I traveled to West Point and saw him graduate for the second time.

I have remained close to Jonny in the two decades since, though I haven't seen him often because he's spent little time on this side of the Atlantic. He served combat tours in Afghanistan and then Iraq, where he suffered a severe back injury when his Humvee was destroyed by an improvised explosive device, a car on the side of the road filled with artillery shells and cans of diesel fuel. Jonny already had back problems; an Army surgeon had tried to exempt him from combat duty, but Jonny refused to let his commander and soldiers down. His injuries from the IED attack made his back much worse and extensive surgery was required. Jonny now lives in pain but continues to soldier on. Since his combat tours he's been stationed in Tbilisi, Georgia, at NATO headquarters in Brussels, where he served as an expert on Russia, and in Germany. Between deployments he returned to the States and obtained a Master's from Harvard in Russian, Eastern European, and Central Asian Studies.

In May 2018 Jonny, by then a lieutenant colonel with hair much grayer than mine, came to Mississippi with his wife Catherine and their four young children and spent a week with Carrie and me. Three of their kids were 10, seven, and four, the same ages that Ann Lowrey, Cliff, and Paul were during the year Jonny lived with us. The Drakes were here not just to see us but also for Jonny to receive the Jackson Prep outstanding alumnus award and give the commencement address in the same auditorium where he had graduated 23 years earlier.

The themes of Jonny's speech were the benefits of learning to overcome adversity and living life with gratitude and humility. To illustrate the importance of gratitude, Jonny spoke of meeting with a village elder while leading a platoon on patrol in Afghanistan on Thanksgiving Day. The man lived in a mud hut with no furniture, no plumbing, and no electricity, just a mat and a prayer rug. When Jonny asked if there was anything he needed, the man gestured to the laughing children outside and said he had a family. He also said he had fields to work and hands to work them. What more could he want? As I listened to Jonny's speech, it occurred to me that he would not be giving it if he had moved to Montana for his senior year.

I am 20 years older than Jonny. It may seem odd to look up to someone who's that much younger than I am, but I look up to Jonny. I rank him among the finest men I've ever known, right up there with Judge Clark and not far below Daddy.

Chapter 25

I love the outdoors and always have. From my earliest years of playing in the creek, the woods, and the vacant lot, I have always preferred to be outside when the weather's nice. When Carrie and I moved to our new home, I built an outdoor shower as well as a swinging bed on the screened porch that I suspended with ropes from the ceiling. I don't know if I got my love for the outdoors from Daddy, but I got it from somewhere. Being a lawyer is not an outdoor job and has kept me inside more than I like, but I've found ways to practice law outside. We have a patio at home, there's one at my firm's office, and I work outside on both whenever I can.

There was no patio at the Trustmark Bank Building where I worked at the Brunini firm for more than 20 years, but Smith Park, which covered a city block across the street from the governor's mansion, was only a short walk away. Scattered throughout the park were small square tables with inlaid tile checkerboards on top and concrete stools on opposite sides. When I had a brief to write or a document to read, I would often work in the park, where I could hear the birds and not the phone. There was only one drawback. I was often approached by panhandlers asking for money. I would give them the change in my pocket or a dollar or two.

One morning in the park I noticed a likely panhandler 20 feet away. He approached gradually, at an angle. I looked down at the brief I was editing, avoiding eye contact, hoping he would leave me alone. He took two more steps and then spoke. "Excuse me, sir." I could no longer ignore him and looked up. He was a middle-aged black man and appeared to be down on his luck. He was wearing frayed jeans, had stains on his shirt, and was holding a tattered paper bag. He almost certainly had not enjoyed the privileges that I had. I waited for his request. Usually they just asked for money, but often they said why they needed it, for food or sometimes for bus fare.

He started by repeating himself. "Excuse me, sir." But then came this: "Do you have time to play a game of chess?" He then opened the paper bag and held it out for me to see that he meant it. There was a chess set inside. If I had been given a thousand guesses about what he would say and a thousand more about what was in the bag, I would have been wrong two thousand times. And I was too surprised to seize the opportunity to take a break from work, play a game of chess, and learn his story. I said I liked chess but was too busy, maybe another time. He said maybe so, smiled, and walked away. I never saw him again.

Life is filled with regrets, both large and small. This one goes in the small column, but in the two decades since that day I've often thought of the man I wrongly assumed was a panhandler. I wish I had taken the time to find out how his life had brought him to Smith Park on a spring morning with a chess set in a paper bag looking for someone to play with him. And I wish I'd played him a game. We might have had little in common, but we had chess, and we might have learned that we had more.

In 1994, the same year Jonny Drake came to live with us, we moved to a new neighborhood that gave me a much better place than Smith Park for spending time outside. The Pearl River, which forms the eastern boundary of the City of Jackson, was only a short walk from our new home. Old-growth trees—beech, oak, sycamore, cypress, and others—cover the flood plain along the river. The woods are filled with white-tailed deer, barred owls, and trails for hiking and biking. On weekends I would often walk from our house to the river, sometimes with children or a dog or both but often alone.

One year, a week before Christmas, I was walking by myself in the woods late on a Sunday afternoon when I came across a boy of seven or eight. He was also alone. This was no place to be half an hour before dark for a child his age, but he didn't seem worried.

He said he'd come to the river with his big brother but hadn't seen him in a while and didn't know where he was. I knew his parents and where they lived and volunteered to walk the boy to the edge of the woods so he would get home by dark.

When I told him the days were getting short and it would be dark soon, he asked me why, so on our short walk together I explained the science of it to him. I described how the Earth tilts on its axis, which determines how many hours of daylight we get and how many hours of night. I told him about the winter solstice, the day on which the tilt of the axis reaches its peak and the Northern Hemisphere has the least sunlight and the most darkness. I said we were only a day or two from the solstice and so this was one of the shortest days of the year.

He was a bright boy and seemed interested, so when I finished the lesson I asked him if he knew what the longest day of the year was. I figured he would say no and then I would tell him about the summer solstice that comes in June every year. But he surprised me. Not only did he know what the longest day of the year was, he was sure of it. When I asked him to tell me, he didn't hesitate. "Christmas Eve," he said. We reached the edge of the woods and I sent him on his way home. I then retraced our steps, rewarded for my good deed with a good story.

Chapter 26

In 1990 I defended the employer in an age discrimination case, *Little v. Republic Refining Ltd.*, before Judge William Barbour, an excellent federal judge in Jackson. The plaintiff, who was 65 by the time the case went to trial, was sympathetic but had very little evidence that he lost his job because of his age. As sometimes happens with a jury, however, sympathy carried the day. After several hours of deliberation the jurors reported that they were deadlocked. Judge Barbour considered declaring a mistrial and ordering us to start all over but, when the plaintiff's lawyer pleaded with him not to, decided to bring the jury back the next morning. After sleeping on it, they returned a verdict for the plaintiff and awarded him nearly $100,000. But Judge Barbour disagreed; he ruled that the evidence did not support the verdict and granted judgment in my client's favor. The plaintiff then appealed and for the first time I got to argue a case in the Fifth Circuit, the court on which I'd clerked for Judge Clark nearly a decade earlier. The three judges who heard the appeal agreed unanimously with Judge Barbour and affirmed his ruling.

The same week the Fifth Circuit published its opinion in the case, Ingalls Shipbuilding, a naval shipyard on the Mississippi Coast and the state's largest employer, lost at trial in a case that was very similar to the case I had lost but then won. Bill Powers, the company's head in-house lawyer, read the opinion in my case and hired me to handle the appeal in the shipyard's case. The Fifth Circuit again decided the case in my client's favor and I was rewarded with a great deal of additional work for the shipyard, including all of its employment cases as well as other business litigation. In the nearly three decades since then, the shipyard has changed owners twice and I've changed firms twice, but our relationship has endured through it all. All told I've handled nearly 300 cases for Ingalls.

Shortly after Bill Powers hired me to handle the appeal in my first shipyard case, he hired a new in-house lawyer, Bobby Ariatti. Bobby and I worked with each other on a number of cases, trying several of them, and learned from our time together that we both loved the outdoors—camping, hiking, and canoeing. We planned several trips, but they all got canceled because of work or weather. In September 1996 we finally got to go on a trip together for the first time.

Near the end of the summer that year, Bobby found out that Southwest Airlines was celebrating its 25th anniversary by offering fares of $25 per leg. We booked flights to Reno and planned a long weekend in Yosemite National Park. In a state park between Reno and Yosemite on the first night Bobby and I ever spent together in a tent, we were victims of a surprise attack at three in the morning. The attacker was the park's sprinkler system. Bobby barely got damp because he woke up immediately and fled, but I was slower to react and got much wetter. Despite the sprinkler attack, or maybe because of it, we had so much fun we decided to make a hiking trip to the mountains of the West an annual event. We've missed very few years since then. The trips with Bobby, who was not my best friend when we started but is now, have been some of the grandest adventures and best times of my life. Daddy camped many more nights than I have, but I've camped in many more beautiful places.

I realized after my first few trips with Bobby how often I told stories about them, about the magnificent places we visited and the funny things that happened to us while we were there. Our second trip was to Glacier National Park in Montana, where a free-range cow attacked the rental car Bobby was driving. Our third was to the Tetons in Wyoming, where a doctor who was with us sewed up Bobby's head on a picnic table after he slipped on the snow-covered trail and landed face down on a rock. The doctor had a suture kit but no anesthesia so Bobby had only Scotch to dull the pain. On the last night of our trip another year, I won a sweatshirt off a man's back shooting pool in a smoky bar. The year after that Bobby's wife threw away his camping equipment when she found out he was breaking a solemn promise not to spend another week of his limited vacation time hiking with me. He spent an entire hot August day in a garbage dump searching for it. I told the stories about our trips so often I decided to write them. My book *Travels with Bobby—Hiking in the Mountains of the American West* was published in 2015.

The satisfaction I got from writing that book led to my decision to write this one. I've always loved stories—telling my stories as well as hearing other people tell theirs—and writing *Travels with Bobby* made me realize how much I love writing them too. I enjoyed deciding what to leave in and what to leave out and how to describe what we saw and did and what happened to us along the way. I believe that preserving good stories is worthwhile and came to believe that my stories about hiking in the mountains with Bobby were worth the time it took to write them. My hope was that people would read them and go to the magnificent places Bobby and I went and see what we saw. Some who have read the book have done exactly that.

Chapter 27

A child who grows up without a dog is deprived of one of the great joys of life. One of the most rewarding benefits of the family privilege I enjoyed as a child was the companionship of dogs. We always had a dog when I was growing up and, with rare exceptions, I've always had at least one ever since. And I'm sure I always will. I love dogs and Carrie loves them too. We would have a dozen if I would let her. She calls our dogs the fur children and treats them like royalty.

My first dog was an Eskimo Spitz named Frisky. He was my constant companion from the time we got him when I was six months old until he was hit by a car for the fifth and final time when I was 11. Fences were less common then and dogs' lives more dangerous.

Frisky was almost killed years earlier in a fight with a boxer twice his size named Snuffy who roamed the neighborhood hunting cats. Our cat Puff, named for the one in Margie's first grade reader, had a litter of kittens in the tiny playhouse Daddy had built for us in our backyard. Before long Snuffy showed up. Nobody was there to chase him away so Frisky stood between him and the playhouse, ready to fight to the death to protect Puff and her kittens. And he almost did. When we got home, Frisky was covered in blood and Snuffy was gone, but the cats were safe. A neighbor who'd witnessed the fight told us about it. Frisky recovered at the vet and returned home to a hero's welcome.

We had three more dogs before I left for college. After Frisky we never had to do anything to get one. They just showed up, Mama fed them, and they stayed. The first two were small black dogs of indeterminate origin and breed named Tiny and Princess. The third was a beautiful blonde shepherd mix named Heidi. Before we could have her spayed, a male Labrador retriever made her acquaintance and she had eight black puppies in the same playhouse where Puff had her kittens. After having each puppy, Heidi left the playhouse and ran out to the street to chase cars before returning to give birth to the next one. She was not the smartest dog.

Josey was the first dog I got for myself. I moved out of the fraternity house at the beginning of my senior year at Ole Miss and rented half of a cheap duplex with two friends on 17th Street in Oxford. Because we now had a place of our own, we needed a dog and I volunteered to get one. I adopted Josey, who was half English shepherd and half Australian shepherd, on October 2, 1978. I know the exact date because it was the day Bucky Dent hit a three-run homer for the Yankees to beat the Red Sox in a one-game playoff to win the American League East.

During my years at Duke Josey roamed the campus, once walking up and down the rows in a law school classroom in the middle of a lecture until she found me. When I was walking with her, students I didn't know would speak to her by name, having read it on her collar. One day a neighbor came home with a report from the Duke–North Carolina soccer game, which had lasted longer than it should have because of Josey. She had somehow managed to get onto the field, which prompted the referees to stop the game until she could be removed. If someone had whistled or called her, she would have come right away and the game could have resumed immediately, but instead the players tried to catch her, which was a mistake. Josey loved nothing more than a game of chase and, though the players were quick, she was quicker and had twice as many legs. She would get low to the ground, wait for them to commit, then evade them. After 15 futile minutes they gave up and she trotted off to a round of applause. Josey was a great athlete and a great dog and much smarter than Heidi.

When our children were young, we decided it would be fun for them to experience having a litter of puppies, so we got my first purebred dog since Frisky, a Welsh corgi puppy we named Maggie. We chose a corgi because I'd read that they had a big dog's personality in a small dog's body. The article didn't mention how much they shed. As planned, we found a male corgi when the time came and Maggie had a litter of seven puppies. They were easy to tell apart because they all had different markings and the children insisted on naming them. Cliff wanted to name one Mary, but there were only two females and Ann Lowrey had named both of them immediately. So Cliff named one of the male puppies Mary. It didn't matter because the names were temporary. We didn't plan to keep any of the puppies and their new owners would give them permanent names, a more appropriate name in Mary's case. Twelve weeks after they were born, we had sold six of the seven. The last one, as fate would have it, was Mary. He was a very sweet puppy and we had all grown attached to him. When our want ad expired with no takers, we decided to keep him.

I then assumed responsibility for persuading Cliff that we needed to change Mary's name. I explained that Mary wasn't a name a self-respecting male dog would want, but Cliff would have none of it. I threw out every option I could think of, traditional dog names like Fido, Spot, and Rover and nontraditional ones, at least for dogs, such as Fred and John. Any male or gender-neutral name would do. Cliff refused to pick one. Mary was Mary and that was that. I then had an epiphany. Why not Murray? Very similar to Mary but a male name. And a unique one. We would have the first ever dog named Murray. Cliff wouldn't budge. We registered the puppy as Cliff's Mister Mary. We could have spelled it Merry and claimed he was named for Merry Brandybuck in *Lord of the Rings*, but it would have been a lie. Mary didn't care one way or the other. He was a wonderful dog and perfectly content with his name.

Years later we bought a lot on a fishing lake north of Jackson and hired Betsy Ann's younger brother to build a cabin. By then we were back to mixed-breed dogs. We had two great ones: Elvis, part Lab, and Bob, part chow. We didn't know the other parts. When we were about to return home from the cabin one Sunday, they disappeared, likely chasing deer they couldn't possibly catch. We looked high and low and called until dark but couldn't find them. We put an ad in the paper and their pictures on telephone poles. We offered a $100 reward. We enlisted the help of the sheriff's department and returned every day to the cabin to continue the search. A week went by and we were about to give up hope, but then one evening my cell phone rang. A man at a hunting camp had the dogs. The camp was 20 miles east of the cabin, across two state highways, an interstate, and a number of wide creeks. When I walked into the camp and sat down, Elvis ran to me, put his head on my leg, and whimpered. The man said that was all the proof he needed. When I tried to give him the hundred dollars, he waved me off and handed me a beer.

Carrie and I were temporarily without a dog when Daddy came to live with us in September 2011, and we decided he needed a companion while we were gone during the day. I had served on the board of directors of an animal shelter in Jackson called CARA, and Carrie and I went there in search of a small housebroken dog that would be good with Daddy and the grandchildren. We came home with Mollie, a gentle cocker spaniel. Daddy loved dogs, and he and Mollie hit it off right away. He would sit in his recliner and throw a tennis ball for her to retrieve and he shared all his meals with her, eating what he wanted and then holding his plate a few inches off the floor for Mollie to eat the rest. He even shared his ice cream, which he ate after dinner every night without fail. It wasn't good for her, but how do you tell your 90-year-old father to stop feeding the dog?

After Daddy died in July 2013, it was Mollie who needed a companion when we were away during the day. She had gone from eating ice cream to dry dog food and from lounging in her favorite chair in the living room to spending her days outside alone in the heat. We went to a Petco near our house where a shelter from Belzoni, a small town in the Mississippi Delta, was having an adoption day. The name of the shelter was Belzoni Animal Rescue Kennel, BARK for short. We walked in the front door of Petco and there stood Buster, a handsome mixed-breed hound dog, much more my style than a cocker spaniel. We brought him home and he and Mollie immediately became fast friends. Carrie spoiled them rotten, making them eggs and bacon every weekend. I gave her a beautiful portrait of them painted by a Tupelo High School classmate one Christmas, and I've been working on a book about them, which will be my third if life goes according to plan.

The idea for the book started with a conversation in our bedroom one Saturday morning that I overheard from the kitchen. I first heard Carrie say something and then heard someone respond in a much higher voice. I was pretty sure nobody else was in the house and I suspected who the someone was. I tiptoed to the bedroom door and caught Carrie in the act. First she said something to Mollie and then, in the higher voice, said something as Mollie. I watched in wonder as the conversation continued, then interrupted and asked what on earth she was doing. Her reaction was not what I expected. I thought she would be embarrassed, but she was indignant. "Channeling the dog, of course," she declared. "You're crazy," I said. "Everybody does it," she responded. "Not everybody," I assured her. Mollie said nothing.

In the weeks after I caught Carrie conversing with our cocker, I asked our dog-loving friends if they channeled their dogs. Some gave me blank stares but, after I explained what I meant, many admitted it, some sheepishly, some forthrightly. With that as precedent, I took to channeling our dogs like a duck to water. Because most of Carrie's talks were with Mollie, most of mine were with Buster. He said the darnedest things. One day Carrie said I needed to write down my conversations with him. The working title of the book is *Bedtime with Buster*. It's not yet a book, but I hope it will be, though it won't be much like this one.

In January 2019 we added a third dog to the family. Carrie decided we should adopt another shelter dog, this time a senior dog. She evidently wasn't satisfied with spoiling Buster, Mollie, and me. A friend posted photos on Facebook of a Wheaten terrier from a shelter on the Mississippi Coast and we drove south the three hours to get her. When we brought her home, we had three old dogs adopted from three different shelters—Mollie from CARA in 2011, Buster from BARK in 2013, and Maddie from the Jackson

County Animal Shelter in 2019. Maddie is sweet and adorable; she has no front teeth so her tongue sticks out involuntarily. She has a crush on Buster and follows him around the house licking his head, but she's been spayed and he's been neutered so licking is all she can do. After we got Maddie, I would take all three dogs for long walks together. By the time we got home, their leashes would be as intertwined as one of Grandma's crocheted placemats.

Carrie loves Buster and Maddie, but there is no doubt about her favorite. Mollie became Carrie's baby the day we brought her home from CARA. The two spent hours together on the couch, with Mollie on her back in Carrie's lap. Mollie was afraid of thunder so when a storm came Carrie would lift her up and put her in the bed to sleep with us. More than once I discovered Mollie in the bed when there was no thunder and she wasn't afraid. When I asked why, Carrie would claim there was a possibility of rain in the forecast. Mollie enjoyed licking Carrie's face and she sat patiently and let Mollie do it. I was not as patient. Carrie had a dozen nicknames of unknown origin for her—Francine, Louisa, Prisserina, Angel Face, and many others. Mollie knew some of them, but the sheer number was overwhelming, especially when Carrie used them in combination.

Several months after Maddie joined our family, Mollie got sick. She sneezed violently, there was an audible rasp when she breathed, and she had a slight nosebleed. The vet prescribed an antibiotic and a steroid, but she got worse instead of better. He then performed a rhinoscopy and discovered what he feared, an inoperable tumor blocking her breathing and pressing against her eye. As we awaited the biopsy results, her condition deteriorated. She stayed in bed with us each night, but even with painkillers she slept little. She turned down eggs and bacon as well as ice cream and peanut butter.

After several days we talked to the kind vet and made the hard decision. He and his assistant came to our house to spare Mollie the stress of a final trip to the clinic. She was the gentlest of dogs and cooperated with the procedure, as she cooperated with all things, and she died in Carrie's arms with Carrie's tears dripping on her head. I buried her in an azalea bed in our front yard and have planted a tree in her honor. It's Mollie's tree. Carrie lay in the bed the night Mollie died staring at the portrait of her and Buster. A friend told me that dogs give you the best days of your life and one of the worst. What a wonderful dog Mollie was.

Writing about my many loyal dogs makes me realize how much they've meant to me and how much they've enriched my life. They've made the hard times easier and the good times better, but losing them has made for some of the worst. There is precious little in all the world better than a good dog.

Chapter 28

Ann Lowrey was a precocious child. She figured things out before other children did. When she was only two, a close friend of ours nicknamed her "the woman grown." I noticed my friends were careless about what they said around their young children. I had to be careful. Ann Lowrey understood.

The first home Betsy Ann and I bought in Jackson was on Meadowbrook Road. Mortgage rates were 14 percent and we couldn't afford much. The house was uninhabitable when we bought it. For more than a year while we fixed it up, we lived in the drafty, uninsulated 400-square-foot garage apartment behind it. The previous occupant of the apartment was a drug dealer. We learned his occupation because his customers occasionally pulled into our gravel driveway looking for him. They were disappointed that he no longer lived there and dismayed that we didn't know where he had gone.

I knew little about remodeling when we started work on the house but a lot by the time we finished. We moved from the garage apartment into the house two months before Ann Lowrey was born. The neighborhood was old, as were most of our wonderful neighbors. A sweet couple, Ruth and Virgil Priester, lived behind us. Sudie Schultz lived across the street. She loved all things purple and wanted a purple house, but her daughter Suellen objected. Sudie waited until Suellen left town, hired painters, and got the house she wanted. Ed and Flavia Helm, who had owned a men's clothing store, lived two doors down from us.

When Ann Lowrey was two, Flavia began requesting her

company on weekday afternoons. They would spend hours in the Helms' kitchen talking while Flavia cooked dinner. Flavia gave Ann Lowrey candy and Ann Lowrey gave Flavia joy in return. One day they walked back to our house and Flavia came inside laughing to report on their conversation. Ann Lowrey had been sitting on the kitchen counter chewing on a Tootsie Roll when she made a pronouncement about their relationship: "I like you, Flavia," she said, "but I love your candy." Ann Lowrey has always been candid, sometimes to a fault.

In the spring of 1987 I took Ann Lowrey to mother's morning out one morning on my way to work. We were in the Toyota pickup I had bought to replace my VW Beetle that was totaled in my wreck on West Street the summer before. Once we were in the carpool line, I let her get out of her car seat. She stood between the bucket seats and studied herself carefully in the rearview mirror. She turned her head from side to side and, without looking at me, said "Daddy, I believe I need to lose a little weight." She was not yet three.

A year later a designer of children's clothes asked if we would allow Ann Lowrey to serve as a model in a fashion show. She was a beautiful girl but, more than that, she was poised, mature, and fearless. We consented and she walked down the runway in the fancy dresses, smiled at the audience, turned, and walked back. Also that year Ann Lowrey was chosen to be the barker in the annual circus at her preschool. She memorized her lines and delivered them flawlessly. No nerves, no fear. Everyone could hear every word. She was never a quiet child. Still isn't.

Two years after that we let Ann Lowrey skip a day of school in the first grade so the two of us could take a train trip to New Orleans. We rode down on Saturday and toured the city on Sunday, riding through the French Quarter in a carriage and out St. Charles to the river in a streetcar. On Monday morning she accompanied me to the Fifth Circuit, the magnificent Italian Renaissance Revival courthouse on Camp Street that is now more than a century old, and watched the argument in *Little v. Republic Refining Ltd.* She sat in the gallery and listened as Mr. Little's lawyer and I presented our clients' positions to the three judges. I would be reluctant to take most six-year-olds to court, but I wasn't reluctant to take her.

Ann Lowrey was very bright and made good grades, though they could have been better. She could have been a straight-A student, but she was always more interested in learning what interested her than in her grade point average. In her senior year of high school two of her classmates came to our house at night so she could help them with calculus. One started college that fall at the University of Virginia, the other at Princeton. Ann Lowrey was the one doing the tutoring, but she attended a less prestigious university. Like Daddy, Betsy Ann, and me, she went to Ole Miss, where she studied in the Sally McDonnell Barksdale Honors College.

Ann Lowrey made good grades in college too, but they were still not her principal focus. She set out to establish a mock trial program in which students from one university act as lawyers and try hypothetical cases against students from others. She had excelled in mock trial in high school and loved it. Some colleges had mock trial teams, but Ole Miss did not. Ann Lowrey got one of her favorite Ole Miss professors, John Winkle, who was a favorite of mine a generation earlier, to lead the program, and she convinced the administration to provide academic credit to students who participated. More than a decade later the program continues to thrive. Ann Lowrey was also very active in St. Peter's Episcopal Church and wrote a regular column for the Ole Miss student newspaper, *The Daily Mississippian*. She had other responsibilities while she was at Ole Miss as well, as you will soon learn.

Ann Lowrey graduated with honors from Ole Miss in 2006 and moved back to Jackson, where she worked at my law firm as a paralegal while she considered where to go to law school. She was admitted to many of the best schools in the country with generous scholarship offers from some, including Duke, but she ultimately decided that law school was not for her. She has instead pursued a career as an educator.

The career came about because of Ann Lowrey's decision to home-school her oldest child. Not long after she started, some other parents approached her and asked if she would start a school that would work together with parents who home-school. After much prayer and study, Ann Lowrey, her husband, and others opened a university-model school. They named it St. Augustine in honor of the theologian who loved education. The school establishes the curriculum, offers courses and activities parents can't provide, and gives students the opportunity to spend time with other children that home-schooled kids often lack.

Ann Lowrey was determined that St. Augustine would be successful, and it has been an extraordinary success. Starting from scratch, it has grown to a student body of 200 and gets larger every year. Younger students attend classes two days a week, older kids three. All have assignments on the off days. The young ones work under the supervision of their parents, who are trained to be co-teachers. The older ones are expected to take ownership of their education and work independently. The school does not believe in infantilizing teenagers. The teachers at the school are dedicated, the students motivated. All children should have such a school. Ann Lowrey does for St. Augustine's students what Daddy did for Troop 12's Scouts. I just write about them.

Betsy Ann and I separated in 2007 and divorced the following year after 29 years of marriage. In the wake of the divorce Ann Lowrey and I experienced a sort of role reversal, with my needing advice and her giving it. After my second post-divorce relationship ended, she said I needed to be more patient, not date just one person at a time, and not get so serious so fast. I agreed but pointed out that I was 52 years old. I wasn't interested in going to bars to meet women or dating women who go to bars to meet men, so finding women to go out with was a challenge. In response she declared that she was signing me up for eHarmony. We sat together at the computer in her living room on a Saturday afternoon in April 2010 and enrolled me.

Two weeks later I was matched on the dating site with Carrie Buck, a beautiful blonde from Hattiesburg, 90 miles south of Jackson. Her profile said she loved reading, music, and wine, saved turtles from the road when practical, and was nearly six feet tall in heels but worth the climb. I immediately emailed her and said

I loved wine and music and had saved many a turtle. I wanted to meet her and promised to bring a book and a ladder. We met for lunch in Hattiesburg in May, soon became inseparable, got engaged in September, and married on New Year's Day. 1/1/11, easy to remember. I still wasn't patient, but this time I was right. I have bestowed on Carrie the title of World's Best Wife and I owe my good fortune to Ann Lowrey. If she had not signed me up for eHarmony, Carrie and I never would have met.

Chapter 29

Music has always been a big part of my life. I love to sing and dance, though my enthusiasm for both far exceeds my ability. When my children were young, I made sure they were exposed to good music. While other kids were listening to NSYNC and the Backstreet Boys, I played the Allman Brothers, Steve Earle, and Van Morrison for Ann Lowrey, Cliff, and Paul. We've also had three generations of bedtime singing in the family. Mama sang to me when she put me to bed, I sang to my children, and now, when the grandchildren stay with us, I sing to them as well. They have their favorites and "Sweet Baby James" is at the top of the list. Since Ann Lowrey was a baby, I've probably sung it nearly as many times as James Taylor has.

In the summer of 1987, when Betsy Ann was pregnant with Cliff, she accompanied me to a seminar at Williams College in western Massachusetts. Ann Lowrey, who had just turned three in May, stayed with friends. The day after the seminar ended, we drove from Williamstown down to Stockbridge, where we toured Norman Rockwell's home, then took the Massachusetts Turnpike to Logan Airport in Boston to catch our flight. We made our connection in Atlanta and got home in time to pick up Ann Lowrey and for me to put her to bed. I sang "Sweet Baby James" to her, as I had many times, and then told her we had just come from the Berkshires and had started our journey home on the turnpike from Stockbridge to Boston. Her eyes got wide. She had no idea the song was about a real place.

Carrie and I love live music especially. Several years ago fellow music lovers told us about house concerts, in which touring artists play in residences for the homeowners and their friends. We thought it might be fun to host a show and discussed the pros and cons, but we didn't come to a decision.

In the summer of 2015, based on a friend's recommendation, we went to a downtown Jackson club to see an excellent folk duo from Baton Rouge, Clay Parker and Jodi James. During a break in the show, emboldened by wine, Carrie told them we wanted them to play a house concert for us. That was news to me, but I didn't object. Three months later they performed for us and our friends. They were wonderful, we decided it would be fun to host a show every month or two, and we've had more than 30 house concerts since then. We have dinner before each show. Carrie makes an entrée and guests contribute appetizers, salads, and desserts. We all donate money to the artists, who almost always stay with us. Carrie cooks a big brunch the next morning before they return to the road and head to the next stop on their tour. The house concerts at Camp Carrie, the name I've given our home, are as much fun as anything we do.

Ann Lowrey has accomplished a great deal, but in my biased opinion her greatest achievement is her four children, my wonderful grandchildren. When Ann Lowrey was young, I would hold her down, tickle her, and relent only when she promised to name her first child for me. She could have claimed coercion, but she kept her promise. Her oldest is Ada Brooks, named for the heroine in Charles Frazier's *Cold Mountain* and me. Ada has two brothers, Eason and Collins, and a baby sister, Elsa Gray, the self-appointed boss of them all. They are all very different and all very special. The first and third, Ada Brooks and Collins, are quiet and thoughtful. Eason and Elsa Gray never met a stranger and never hush. Collins likes to come to our house to escape from the noise at his. Elsa Gray keeps talking even when everyone else has left the room.

One or more of the grandchildren often come with their parents to our house concerts. At one, while everyone else danced, Ada Brooks played Scrabble on her iPhone. At another, while no one else danced, Elsa Gray did pirouettes in the aisle. Eason wore the blue blazer we'd given him for Christmas to one concert and volunteered to greet guests at the door. When Collins comes, he sits quietly and enjoys the music but speaks only when spoken to.

The little people, as Carrie calls them, are a joy. She is their favorite. We have a dinner date with each of them every quarter and see all of them every chance we get. They live only 20 minutes from us. We love our home, but if Ann Lowrey moved away with the little people, there would be no deliberation. We would sell Camp Carrie, pack our things, and follow.

Chapter 30

Ann Lowrey has always been strong-willed and independent. These are good qualities most of the time, but not always. A girl's early teen years are often difficult—a school counselor once told me that ninth-grade girls are the meanest people in the world—and Ann Lowrey's were no exception. She was disobedient and disrespectful. She tried to avoid going to school and demanded that we transfer her to a new one. She ran away from home, though she made it only to a Waffle House two miles away. She quit studying and her grades declined. She rejected all authority figures, especially Betsy Ann and me. Appeals to reason failed. Threats of consequences failed. Actual consequences failed. Through the eighth grade Ann Lowrey had been a model child—kind, brilliant, popular. Then, suddenly, she was unbearable.

We laugh about it now and call it the Period of Demonic Possession, but there was nothing funny about it at the time. But then one day it stopped. The hormones stopped raging, the demons went away, and we had our daughter back. We enjoyed Ann Lowrey's last two years of high school, when our house served as the gathering place for her and her many friends. In 2002 she graduated, left for Ole Miss, and the house became much quieter.

In the fall of the following year, when Ann Lowrey was a sophomore, there came a time when I was thankful for her strong will and independence. She was having lunch one day in the student union with a friend from the honors college and decided not to get one of her favorites. Instead, for the first time ever, she ordered a tuna salad sandwich. Her friend looked at her, reminded her that she didn't like tuna, and said she must be pregnant. The friend was joking, but Ann Lowrey started thinking. Being pregnant would sure explain a lot, but how could it be? She was on the pill. After lunch she went to a drug store and bought a home pregnancy test, went back to her room, and followed the directions on the label. The test was positive. She first called her friend with the news. Then she tracked down her boyfriend and told him in person. They were in love, or at least thought they were, and had talked about spending their lives together. But this was not part of the plan.

I spent most of the week before Halloween that year taking depositions in St. Louis, where another lawyer and I happened to take a driving tour through the campus of Washington University on the way to dinner one night. The last deposition ended on Thursday and I headed to the airport, where I called my secretary to check in. She told me to call home right away. When Betsy Ann answered, she said there was a serious problem with one of the children. I asked which one and what. She said she would rather discuss it in person. I said I would rather know now. She resisted. Finally, after I threatened not to come home if she didn't tell me, she broke the news that Ann Lowrey was pregnant. And there was more. Ann Lowrey and her boyfriend had already gone to see his parents and told them. His dad had hugged her and said welcome to the family, but his mother was not receptive. That night Ann Lowrey overheard the woman tell her son, "If you threaten to leave her, she'll do the right thing." He did as he was told. By the time I called home from St. Louis, he'd made the threat, Ann Lowrey had rejected it, and he'd washed his hands of her.

Ann Lowrey drove home from Oxford by herself on Thursday and was there when I arrived. In the space of three days she had found out she was pregnant, and the young man she thought was the love of her life had demanded that she have an abortion and then broken up with her when she refused. She slept in the bed with us that night. She was pitiful.

But not for long. Betsy Ann and I had planned to spend the weekend with friends at a state park on Sardis Lake outside Oxford and go to the Ole Miss–South Carolina football game. Ann Lowrey decided there was no reason for us to change our plans and agreed to spend the weekend with us. On Friday afternoon we drove to Sardis and checked into a cabin. Soon after we arrived, Ann Lowrey's now ex-boyfriend called and said the two families needed to meet, which meant she needed to come back to Jackson on Sunday. She said no, she had classes on Monday and was not returning to Jackson. If he and his parents wanted to meet, they could come to north Mississippi before Betsy Ann and I returned to Jackson. I patted her on the leg.

We had a great weekend with our friends. I had met two of them on the trail in Glacier National Park on one of my hiking trips with Bobby and they had just moved from San Francisco to Franklin, Tennessee. They had spent little time in the South and appreciated Southern hospitality and the beautiful Ole Miss campus.

On Sunday, shortly after they left, Ann Lowrey's ex arrived at Sardis with his parents. They sat on one side of a picnic table with him in the middle. We sat on the other side with Ann Lowrey in the middle. The reason they came, the purpose of the meeting, soon became clear. They were desperate for Ann Lowrey to have an abortion and willing to say anything to get their way. Their son, whom we soon took to calling Bio in recognition of the sum total of his contribution to his child, said he would provide no support whatsoever, emotional or financial, if Ann Lowrey persisted in her decision to have the baby. He also questioned whether the baby was even his. Ann Lowrey just shook her head. His father said they were concerned about their legacy and declared that Ann Lowrey should not want to bring a bastard into the world. He actually said that. I told him not to use that word again but otherwise didn't say much. I was too shocked and too disgusted. They obviously had no concern for Ann Lowrey, much less for the baby who would be their first grandchild if they didn't get their way. Their goals were entirely selfish—to avoid embarrassment and escape responsibility. The meeting was short and they headed back south.

Ann Lowrey was more angry than hurt. Her attitude was good riddance. She now wanted nothing from Bio, no financial support or anything else. She just wanted him gone. Betsy Ann agreed.

My position was just the opposite. I vowed that he was going to put my grandchild through Harvard Medical School. His mother, whom we started calling something much worse than Bio, said little at our picnic-table meeting. But later, after their abortion effort had failed, she wrote me and urged me to persuade Ann Lowrey to give the baby up for adoption. Both Ann Lowrey and her son were gifted, she wrote, and they should be able to plan their futures "unencumbered." This led to a third nickname. For a time we called the baby, whom Ann Lowrey soon found out was a girl, the Little Encumbrance.

Their adoption strategy, like the abortion ploy, was unsuccessful. I did not try to control Ann Lowrey's decision, but I did tell her we had the resources to help her and there was no reason she couldn't keep her baby. Ann Lowrey had received a scholarship from Ole Miss and her daughter could be on scholarship from me. I also reminded her that adoption would not guarantee a bright future for her child, that not all adoptive parents could be as wonderful as the ones we knew. So Ann Lowrey decided she would have her baby and keep her baby. Friends told us they admired us for standing by her and supporting her, but it never occurred to me to do anything else.

We initially thought Ann Lowrey would come home from Ole Miss at Christmas break and live with us until the baby was born, but she found out she wasn't due until mid-June, so she stayed in school through the spring semester. She was not only strong-willed and determined but, unlike most 19-year-old girls at Ole Miss, she didn't much worry about what other people thought. She focused on her studies, trudging up the hill from her dorm to classes. By the time she took her last exam in May, she was eight months pregnant. I don't know how Bio felt about having his pregnant ex-girlfriend on campus, but I know how he should have felt.

We loaded up and headed to the hospital on the morning of June 17. The labor went fast. When the doctor checked on Ann Lowrey's progress just before noon, he said it was time. I tried to escape from the delivery room, but he said it was too late. I was stuck. I looked down at my phone and read emails until Ada Brooks

Eason came into the world screaming. First they wrapped her in a blanket and handed her to Ann Lowrey, then they gave her to me. When I took her to the newborn nursery to be weighed and examined, the nurses thought I was her father. I was old to be her father but young to be her grandfather and there was nobody else in sight. When the nurse put Ada on the scale, she weighed seven pounds and almost five ounces. I asked the nurse to list her at seven pounds, four ounces, because that's how much I weighed when I was born, but she was a stickler and rounded up instead of down.

Most newborn babies are red, wrinkled, and unattractive. Not Ada Brooks, who was beautiful from the beginning. But her first days weren't easy for her or for us. Shortly after she came home from the hospital, she developed stomach pains. She would cry until she was exhausted and we were too. The one thing that seemed to soothe her was being outside in the heat, so I would take her for walks in the neighborhood when I got home from work. It was mid-summer in Mississippi and the heat was oppressive. I would sweat, but she would finally stop crying. And when she did, I would stop by our neighbors' homes to show off our beautiful baby. A woman who had nothing but sons fell in love with her. I soon gave her a new nickname. She was no longer the Little Encumbrance. She was now the Grand Prize. I kept calling her that until she learned to talk and I taught her to call herself that. She pronounced the r's as w's: Gwand Pwize. I thought it was adorable, but Ann Lowrey did not. She didn't want her daughter claiming to be the grand anything and made us both stop.

By August, when Ada Brooks was two months old, her stomach pains were gone and Ann Lowrey headed back to Oxford with her. Every weekday morning Ann Lowrey went to class after dropping Ada off at the Mother Goose. She was adored by the staff there, including a woman from Pakistan who called her "the baby Ada." Being a single mother is difficult and exhausting, but millions of women do it. With help from her many friends, one of whom she later married, Ann Lowrey thrived. Her years at Ole Miss were much more challenging than mine, but I believe she had just as much fun. She came home often and we made regular trips to

Oxford. As I was walking around the Oxford town square one afternoon with Ada Brooks on my shoulders, I was stopped twice by strangers who told me she was the most beautiful child they had ever seen.

Chapter 31

Not long after the unpleasant picnic-table meeting with Bio and his parents at Sardis Lake, it became my responsibility to tell Daddy and Ann Lowrey's brothers that she was pregnant and that Bio was no longer in the picture. Paul was 13, an age not known for empathy, and his first concern was that he would be embarrassed to have a pregnant sister. But he got over it quickly, became a doting uncle, and still is. Cliff, who was 16, reacted with anger. When I told him what Bio had done, Cliff threatened to kill him. He didn't call him by name but instead used a two-word expletive he'd never used in my presence before. I chastised him for his language but was proud of him for being loyal to his sister. Daddy, predictably, was not judgmental but expressed concern for Ann Lowrey and the baby. The child needs a father, he said more than once.

The percentage of children born out of wedlock in America has skyrocketed in the last six decades, from less than five percent in 1960 to 40 percent today. The increase has reduced the stigma unwed mothers faced in previous times, which is for the good. Dealing with an unplanned pregnancy and a newborn baby is hard enough without being shamed and treated as a pariah. But the increasing number of out-of-wedlock births has come with enormous costs for society, for the single mothers who bear the burden of raising their children alone, and for the millions of children who grow up in fatherless homes. By every measure—academic achievement, criminality, poverty, health, and others—children raised in two-parent homes fare far better than those raised without fathers. Poverty is exceedingly rare among couples who finish school, get a job, get married, and have children in that order. That is not a criticism of single mothers, who often go to heroic efforts for their children, but a reflection of the fact that Daddy was right. Children need fathers.

And before long Ada Brooks had one. Paul Forster was Ann Lowrey's friend from the honors college who had joked about her being pregnant when she ordered a tuna salad sandwich. After Bio abandoned her, she and Paul became very close. He took her to the doctor before Ada Brooks was born and babysat for her after. When I asked Ann Lowrey about their relationship, she insisted they were just friends, but I wondered why a young man at Ole Miss, which is famous for its beautiful women, would choose to spend his time with a single mother and her baby. But he remained a constant presence, I kept asking, and Ann Lowrey kept insisting.

But in the spring of their junior year her answer changed. They had started out as friends but were now more than that. They got engaged in the fall of their senior year and married the following April. Ada Brooks, who would turn two in June, was the flower girl in their wedding at St. Peter's in Oxford. Before the ceremony Betsy Ann and I practiced with her, showing her how to scatter the flower petals from her basket as she walked down the aisle. The three of us then picked the petals back up and returned them to the basket. Ada learned her part too well. Ann Lowrey and I were in the foyer alone waiting for the wedding march, which would be our cue to start down the aisle, when we heard the congregation laughing. Ada Brooks, just as we'd rehearsed, had scattered the petals as she walked down the aisle. Then, also as we'd rehearsed, she'd turned around, headed back up the aisle, and picked them up. There had been three Margarets in the family—Momie, Mama, and Margie—and now we had three Pauls—my daddy, my son, and my son-in-law. To avoid confusion, on Christmas present tags and otherwise, we called them Big Paul, Little Paul, and Paul the Groom.

Ann Lowrey and Paul the Groom graduated from the honors college two weeks after the wedding. The new family then moved to Jackson, where Betsy Ann and I hosted an outdoor reception for them. Our favorite local band performed and I danced with both my daughter and my granddaughter. Near the end of the party, after too many friends had brought me too many drinks, I took the stage and sang "The Weight" by The Band. I remembered most of the words.

Four months after Ada's second birthday we all went to the Mississippi State Fair on a perfect October evening. As we walked down the midway surrounded by bright lights, Ada looked from side to side, taking it all in. We came to a tall pink slide, its top 30 feet off the ground, and Ada declared that she wanted to slide. I volunteered to pick her up, carry her to the top, and slide with her, but she didn't want to be carried. We climbed the stairs side by side holding hands and then slid down together with her sitting in front of me. I couldn't see her face, but I could see the smiles on the faces of those who were watching from the ground and could. When we reached the bottom, Ada Brooks hopped up, beaming, and said, "Go again."

For the next half hour, until we were all exhausted, we took turns climbing the stairs and sliding down with Ada. She got tired too and allowed herself to be carried to the top, but she did not tire of sliding. Each time when she reached the bottom, she stood up and said, "Go again." Nothing else. She would have kept sliding all night. Strangers walking along the midway noticed the beautiful, joyful child coming down the slide and stopped to watch. I couldn't help but think of Bio and his parents, our picnic-table meeting three Octobers before, and what they were missing now. I thought to myself, *What foolish, foolish people.*

Ann Lowrey and Betsy Ann got their way about Bio and he got his way too. He never provided Ann Lowrey with any support, emotional or financial. Ada Brooks may go to Harvard Medical School—she's more than bright enough—but Bio will not pay for it. He relinquished his parental rights after Paul and Ann Lowrey got married and I prepared the legal papers for Paul to adopt Ada. When the adoption was finalized, she ceased being Ada Brooks Eason and became Ada Brooks Forster.

Paul is the only father Ada's ever known and he's a fine one. During their last two years at Ole Miss, he and Ann Lowrey often drove with the baby Ada the 50 miles to Tupelo and spent Sunday afternoons with Daddy. Ann Lowrey would do laundry and Paul would try to persuade Daddy to let him help in the yard or around the house. Daddy was reluctant, but one Sunday he said Paul could hold the ladder while he climbed it to clean out the gutters on the roof. Paul insisted they swap roles. It took some convincing, but Daddy relented and held while Paul climbed. Paul was 21, Daddy 84.

In John Irving's famous novel *The Cider House Rules*, Wilbur Larch is the elderly doctor who runs the orphanage in St. Cloud, Maine. When young orphan Homer Wells decides he wants to stay at the orphanage permanently, Dr. Larch gives him one rule to live by. Dr. Larch instructs him, "Homer, I expect you to be of use." Daddy lived his life to be of use. So does Paul the Groom.

I was barred from calling Ada Brooks the Grand Prize long ago, but she still is. She is beautiful, with curls women would pay thousands for, as well as brilliant. She skipped one grade and could skip all the rest if her parents would let her. Two hundred years to the day after Abraham Lincoln was born, she was the barker in her preschool circus. It was 20 years after her mother played the same role in the same circus at the same preschool. Ada was not as loud but just as flawless. She is also kind and considerate to all, patient with her brothers, and guilty of spoiling Elsa Gray. She calls me Papa, the name I chose for myself.

Like her parents, Ada is curious and loves to learn. When she was six or seven and Eason three or four, I took the two of them for a walk in a state park along the Pearl River in Jackson. At a curve in the river we stopped so they could play in the dirt. After a few minutes of digging, Ada looked up at me and asked, "Papa, am I taller than a penguin?" I have no idea what made her think of the height of penguins while she was playing in the dirt. Nor did I know the answer to her question, but I said I figured she was shorter than some but taller than others. With a quick internet search I confirmed that it was true. Now she's taller than all of them, even the Emperor, the tallest penguin on Earth. She's also taller than her mother and both of her grandmothers.

Some years later Bio and his wife moved into a neighborhood

near the one where Carrie and I live. Between the two is the Natchez Trace as well as a paved hiking trail that runs through the woods alongside it. Several times when I was walking Mollie and Buster on the trail I spotted Bio on the trail running toward me. I looked at him, but he avoided eye contact and picked up the pace until he passed me. I had mixed emotions when I saw him. Part of me wanted to get a taser, zap him as he ran by, and laugh as he rolled down the hill beside the trail. But the other part wanted to stop him, thank him for my wonderful granddaughter, and shake his hand. I did neither. One day I passed him and his wife pushing a stroller. I wanted to ask her if she knew her baby had a big sister, but I didn't do that either.

Chapter 32

Before Ada Brooks was born, Ann Lowrey was staunchly pro-choice. She chose to have her baby, but she believed women should have the right to choose abortion. But after Ada was born, she changed her mind. She decided that an unborn baby's right to live must take precedence over a woman's right to choose. It's understandable that having and holding a baby, especially the baby Ada, had that effect on her.

Shortly after moving to Jackson, Ann Lowrey was encouraged to submit an essay to an organization called Feminists for Life about her opinion on the subject and her experience of becoming a single mother while she was in college. The organization, which was founded in 1972, is dedicated to eliminating the root causes that drive women to have abortions, primarily lack of resources and support. Feminists for Life is based on the belief that abortion is the result of society's failure to meet the needs of women in the workplace, school, home, and society. They regard abortion as a symptom of the struggles women face, not a solution to them. Feminists for Life focuses many of its efforts on college campuses, encouraging universities to include maternity care in health plans and offer child care and flexible class scheduling. The organization also assists new mothers who are not able to parent with placing their babies for adoption. Their overall vision is a world in which pregnancy, motherhood, and birth motherhood are all fully accepted and supported and in which there are no abortions because there is no need for them.

After reading Ann Lowrey's essay, Feminists for Life asked her to speak to students about the two choices she made when she was nineteen—to have her baby and keep her baby—and flew her to universities to share her experiences. She also gave a speech for the organization to an audience of more than 5,000 in January 2008 at the March for Life in Washington. Ann Lowrey was no longer the circus barker, but she was still fearless.

Daddy in the Navy

Marjory and Mama

January 21, 1950

Margie and me

The four of us

Daddy and me when he was grand marshal of the
Tupelo Christmas parade in 2003

The champion sleeper

Julie in the middle with her cousins

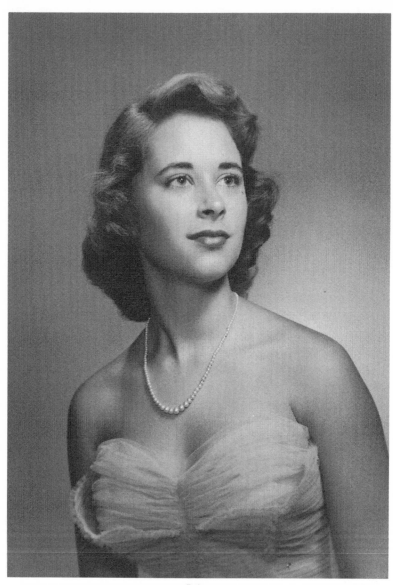

Julie

April 25, 1964

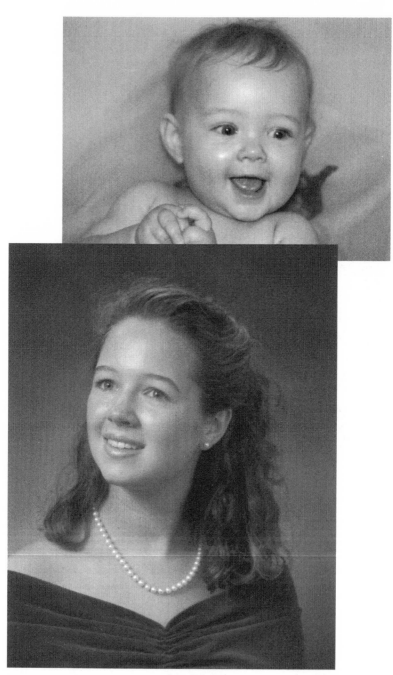

Ann Lowrey

Ada Brooks

Ada Brooks and Carrie on January 1, 2011

The little people

Julie and Ada Brooks at the same age

Julie and me at the same age

Chapter 33

"I can't believe we found you."
"What is this about?"
"An inheritance"
"Tell me more."

And so we return to where we began, to the phone call in June 2004. When I asked the New Orleans lawyer to tell me more, she said I would need to get the details from Ben Faulkner, a lawyer in Tulsa. I knew I was born in New Orleans and that Mama and Daddy adopted me from there, so I asked if this had something to do with one of my birth parents. It seemed like a long shot nearly five decades after my birth, but it was my only theory. She said yes and was glad I had brought it up, that children who were adopted in that era were often never told they were adopted. They were allowed to go through life thinking they were their parents' biological children.

I was aware of one such child in Tupelo. A classmate of Margie's found her adoption papers tucked away in a closet at the worst possible age, when she was a teenager. The discovery was traumatic for her and she made it even more traumatic for her parents. Mama and Daddy were wiser than they were. They told Margie and me we were adopted when we were very young. I can't remember not knowing. In fact, I probably knew I was adopted even before I understood what it meant. And it never bothered me. When you're adopted, you know your parents want you. I had wonderful parents, and I knew they wanted me. And before the call from the lawyer in New Orleans, I had never done anything to research my origin or try to find either of my birth parents.

I also rarely thought about the fact that I was adopted, though from time to time something or someone would remind me. When I was growing up, people who didn't know I was adopted would say I looked like, or didn't look like, one of my parents. I look like neither. An older member of the First Methodist Church once said she thought I resembled Dr. Brooks. I look even less like him. When I started school, I realized that Mama and Daddy were a decade older than most of my friends' parents. The age difference reminded me that I did not become my parents' child the way my friends became theirs. Once or twice a family acquaintance observed that I was Daddy Cliff's only son's only son and it would be up to me to have a son to carry on the family name. I wondered if I could do that, if I qualified. I never felt I didn't belong or was different from my cousins, but the prospect of carrying on the family name reminded me that Daddy and his parents, sisters, nieces, and nephews were all the same flesh and blood. I was not.

When I got older, there were occasional reminders. Tupelo is more than 300 miles north of New Orleans. We rarely traveled to a big city when I was growing up, but when we did it was usually to Memphis and never to New Orleans. As a result, the first time I returned to the city where I was born was 19 years after Mama and Daddy brought me home from there in 1957. It was my sophomore year at Ole Miss and some of my fraternity brothers and I headed south for the annual football game against LSU scheduled for the last Saturday in October. The game was in Baton Rouge, but we decided to make the most of the weekend by staying in New Orleans. After checking into our hotel Friday afternoon, four to a room, my roommate Hank Aiken and I walked down Bourbon Street. He was from Jackson, just three hours from New Orleans, and it was very familiar to him. But not to me. It was like nothing I'd ever seen.

Lured by a two-for-one happy hour, we walked into a bar, pulled up two stools, and ordered beers. You could buy beer when you were

18 then. A woman who was wearing very little was dancing on the bar right in front of us. It was also like nothing I'd ever seen. Her dance moves were riveting, but she was so close that we could see the age around her eyes. It appeared she was nearing the end of her career. Hank knew my history, that I was born in New Orleans and given up for adoption there. He also knew I wasn't troubled by it in the least. Without taking his eyes off the dancer, he nudged me with his elbow and said, "She's got your eyes."

Whenever I applied for an insurance policy and was asked to give my family medical history, I would plead ignorance and say I was adopted. One agent wouldn't take adoption for an answer. She insisted that I disclose everything I knew about Mama, Daddy, and Margie and recorded my responses in detail. She noted on the application that I was adopted only because I insisted.

When I first held Ann Lowrey after she was born, I was struck by the fact that she was the first blood relative I had ever seen. Nearly 20 years later Bio's mother, who is also an adoptee, cited the fact that we were both adopted by loving parents when she tried to persuade me to persuade Ann Lowrey to give her baby up for adoption. I did not take her advice. Adoption may be the best option in many cases, but not in Ann Lowrey's. She was mature and responsible, we had the resources to help her, and we wanted to do so. Like me, Ann Lowrey was the beneficiary of family privilege, and there was no reason she couldn't keep her child. And it was the right decision. She's a wonderful mother and Ada Brooks is the Grand Prize.

After Daddy turned 80 but was still hiking and camping with the Scouts, several people who didn't know I was adopted told me I was lucky, that I had excellent genes. Sometimes I would take the time to explain that I didn't have Daddy's genes, but sometimes I just agreed and let it go. At least in terms of longevity, his genes were far better than mine. I have now lived longer than my birth mother and both of her parents, but for most of my life I didn't know who they were, much less that none of them lived past 60.

Occasionally I would hear about adoptees who were trying to find their birth parents. I was curious but never had a burning desire to find mine. Maybe it was because nothing seemed to be missing. There was no void to fill. I also thought Mama and Daddy might be hurt if I began a quest to find my birth parents. So I never did. And the truth is I never would have. But now, without ever searching, I had been found.

Chapter 34

I n the days after I spoke to the lawyer who left a message for Daddy, I learned the details of the story from Ben Faulkner in Tulsa. It was Ben who gave me the news that Julie Francis was my birth mother and who told me about her family. He also explained why a court in New Orleans had ordered a nationwide search for me. Ben and I discussed the details of Sidney Davis's will, the trusts he established, and the trust indenture Julie and Sid signed after Betty died. Ben said the indenture was never revoked, but the oil and gas wells in the trust were nonetheless treated as if Julie owned them outright when she died. Her nephews, the sons of Sandy Buell, thus inherited them under the terms of her will. Sid then acquired them from the Buell brothers.

Ben also explained all that had happened in the 18 years since Julie's death that led to my being found. Though Sid had acquired the oil and gas wells, the land records showed they were still owned by the Sidney H. Davis Testamentary Trust C. Changing the records to put the title in Sid's name or the name of his own family trust would have been complicated and expensive and at the time seemed unnecessary. Throughout the 1990s the revenues and royalties from the wells were paid to Sid and his family. There was no dispute about who should get them and thus no pressing need to correct the land records. Because Sid didn't have title to the wells, however, he couldn't transfer them. He couldn't sell them or give them to his children or to charity. The actions taken to change the title are what led to my being found.

By the end of the 1990s the original trustees named in both

Sidney's will and the trust indenture—Sidney's three children in the former and family lawyer Fenelon Boesche in the latter—had all died. Both documents named First National Bank and Trust Company of Tulsa as successor trustee. That bank no longer existed, but the successor trustee also had a successor, Bank One Trust Company. Bank One wanted Sid's banking business and offered to help fix the problem with the title to the wells.

Though the bankers no doubt wanted to give Sid what he requested, they also wanted to avoid liability for making a mistake. A lawyer at the bank studied the relevant documents to make sure everything was in order and discovered that changing the title was not simply a matter of preparing and filing the necessary paperwork. The issue was more complicated than that. The problem was the language in Sidney's will, which did not provide that the assets in the trust would go to Julie's estate or the beneficiaries of her will when she died. To the contrary, if Julie was deceased when any of the principal in the trust was to be distributed to her, Sidney's will provided that the trust would terminate immediately and everything would go to her "issue," which meant her children. And all the assets were still held in trust when Julie died in 1986.

Julie had no children with either of her husbands and, so far as nearly all the world knew, no children at all. But the will she signed in Aspen in 1978, the will Lewis Bettman tracked down after her death, included a provision that was a revelation to almost all of Julie's friends and relatives. Although she left the bulk of her estate to Mark Hutchison if they were still married and to Sandy's sons if they were not, she directed that one dollar apiece would go to two other male relatives. She left one of the dollars to Sid, noting that their mother had already generously provided for him. Regarding the other dollar and the other male relative, Julie's will stated:

```
In July 1957, in New Orleans, Lou-
isiana, I gave birth, out-of-wedlock,
to a male child who was subsequently
adopted by a person or persons unknown
to me. I give and bequeath to my unknown
```

son, the sum of One Dollar ($1.00) if
his identity and place of residence can
be determined without undue effort and
expense by my Executor.

In July 1957 Julie was only 18 years old, exactly half as old as
Mama. It was the summer after Julie started her freshman year at
Washington University, which I had toured just months before
Daddy got the call from the lawyer in New Orleans.

Chapter 35

After Julie died and her will was found, executor Lewis Bettman did not try to find her son to give him the dollar. Nobody knew who or where he was and, for a dollar, any effort to find him would have been "undue." But from the two wills—Julie's and Sidney's—the lawyer at Bank One would have seen that Julie had a child, the son born in July 1957, and that he had a potential claim to the trust. For its own protection the bank decided to let a judge resolve the issue.

In 2001 Bank One filed a lawsuit in Tulsa asking the court to determine the rights of all the interested parties, including Julie's son. Because my identity was still unknown, I was referred to in the lawsuit as Baby Boy Francis even though I turned 44 the year it was filed. Sid's lawyers argued in response to the suit both that Julie's son would never be found and that he had no rights to the trust. Julie's nephews were also brought into the case because whether they ever owned the assets that they inherited from Julie and that Sid acquired from them was now being called into question. To protect the rights of Baby Boy Francis, the judge in Tulsa appointed Ben Faulkner to act as his guardian.

After accepting the appointment, Ben studied the two wills and other documents and concluded that his unknown client might well have a valid claim. And the claim, which was to oil and natural gas wells in 13 states spanning the country from Georgia to Wyoming, might be worth millions. But there were two obstacles, one legal and one practical. As a legal matter, the claim could be both valid and valuable, but only to the person who owned it. Without him it was worthless. And neither Ben nor anyone else knew the identity of Julie's son, what had become of him, or even if he was still alive. As a practical matter, until and unless Julie's son could be found, Ben did not have a paying client. But the claim looked to be substantial so Ben decided to pursue the matter. He began his quest to identify and find his client.

All Ben had to go by—the only proof Julie's son existed—was the provision in her will. Not only that, but the search was for someone who was born more than four decades before Ben started looking. Julie's son was born 21 years before she signed the will in Aspen, and another 23 years passed before Ben was appointed to try to find him. Ben knew only that the baby was a boy who was born in New Orleans in July 1957 and was adopted by someone. There was much more Ben didn't know. He didn't know the baby's name, either before or after his adoption, his exact date of birth, or when he was adopted. Nor did he know the identity of the baby's adoptive parents or where they lived. The couple could have been anyone from anywhere and the adoption occurred long before records were computerized or the internet existed.

Ben started his search by seeking the Louisiana court records for the adoption. The couple who adopted Julie's son might not still be alive, but identifying them would be the easiest way to find him. In response to Ben's request, however, the Louisiana officials refused to turn over the adoption records or provide any helpful information. They took the position that everything about the adoption must be kept strictly confidential. This was different, Ben argued, because the adoptee might have a viable claim to the trust established by his great-grandfather. Also, because his birth mother had died 15 years earlier, there was no longer any need for confidentiality. The court officials were unpersuaded.

Ben did not give up but instead set out to find a Louisiana lawyer to challenge their decision. He ultimately retained New Orleans lawyer Edith Morris, who filed a lawsuit on behalf of Baby Boy Francis in the Juvenile Court of Orleans Parish. There were now two lawsuits in two states with two lawyers not getting paid by a client whose identity and location remained a mystery. Like his adoptive parents, he could have been anyone from anywhere.

And he also could have died decades earlier when he jumped off a waterfall on a friend's back at Pickwick Lake or when he wrecked his Volkswagen Beetle on West Street in Jackson 10 summers later.

The lawsuits, like most lawsuits, were not resolved quickly. Edith was successful in the first round; the judge in the Juvenile Court ordered disclosure of the adoption file. But the Louisiana officials, still citing confidentiality, still refused to turn them over. Edith then took the matter to the Louisiana Court of Appeals and requested a second order requiring the officials to comply with the first. She was again successful, but the officials again did not comply. They instead appealed to the Louisiana Supreme Court, the highest court in the state. Years passed with no resolution.

Ben and Edith still had no paying client and by all rights she could have declined to respond to the appeal, but she did not. She filed a brief and again argued that the adoption file should be turned over so that Julie's son could be identified and stake his claim to the oil and gas wells his great-grandfather had owned. Before the Supreme Court could rule, however, the judge in Oklahoma issued an order in the suit filed by the bank. The suit was three years old, Ben had not yet found Julie's son, and the issue could not remain unresolved indefinitely. The bank was entitled to a ruling, as were Sid Smith and the Buell brothers. The judge scheduled a hearing on June 30, 2004, which became Ben's deadline to find Baby Boy Francis. The litigation would not be allowed to last as long as *Jarndyce and Jarndyce.*

Ben beat the deadline but just barely. The Louisiana Supreme Court affirmed the ruling of the Court of Appeals and ordered the identity of Julie's baby to be disclosed. There was no higher court to which the officials could appeal so now they had to comply. Clara Butler, the Director of Adoptions for the Orleans Parish Juvenile Court, was responsible for searching the court files for Julie's son. This was not a simple undertaking. The adoption files from the late 1950s were not on any computer and had to be searched by hand. Adding to the difficulty, the files were maintained in the name of the adoptive parents, not the name of the birth mother, and nobody knew who had adopted Baby Boy Francis. Nor were the files maintained by birth date. Julie's will stated that her baby was born in July 1957, but when he was adopted was unknown. Butler's only option was to go through the files one at a time looking for Julie Francis and her baby boy.

But in one of the files—the one labeled Paul and Margaret Eason—she found them. In the file were two birth certificates, the original and a replacement. The original identified the mother as Julia Francis and her baby as Scott Francis. The replacement identified the parents as Paul and Margaret Eason, their baby as Paul Brooks Eason. In all other respects the two certificates were identical. Both stated that the baby was born in Methodist Home Hospital in New Orleans on July 3, 1957, and that he weighed seven pounds, four ounces.

It had taken three years and proceedings in four courts in two states to identify Julie's son, but finding him was easy. The street address for Paul and Margaret Eason on the replacement birth certificate, 1505 Rogers Drive in Tupelo, Mississippi, was for the home where they lived in 1957 and where I grew up. In June 2004, when my adoption file was located, Daddy still lived there. The search took but two calls and the first was to directory assistance. The lawyer got Daddy's number and called him, Daddy called me, and in the space of a few days I learned the whole story.

I was initially reluctant to pursue a claim to the assets in the trust. Julie had given birth to me, but Mama and Daddy were my parents. And Julie had left her estate to relatives she knew and loved —Sandy's sons—not to the son she hadn't seen since days after he was born. But Ben, who had finally found the client he had been looking for all this time, persuaded me to reconsider. He pointed out that the question was not what Julie wanted to do with her assets but what her grandfather wanted to do with his. And what he wanted, if there were still assets in the trust when Julie died, was for them to go to her *issue*—to me. Sidney wanted to keep his money in the family, as Lee Farnham later told me, and I was his great-grandson. And it was possible that Sidney knew about me when he directed that the assets would go to Julie's issue. I was four and a half when he signed his will in January 1962. Betty or Julie may well have told him about me. In fact, he may have arranged for Julie to go to New Orleans when she was pregnant. He had contacts in the oil business there.

So I agreed to pursue the claim and Ben and I agreed that he would represent me. Just days before the June 30 deadline set by the Oklahoma court, Ben filed a pleading disclosing to the judge and the other lawyers that Baby Boy Francis at long last had been found and that he was a lawyer in Jackson, Mississippi, named Brooks Eason.

Chapter 36

The days following the revelation that Julie was my birth mother were filled with more revelations. I was curious about the dollar Julie had left me. If Julie didn't want me to share in her estate, why leave me a dollar? And why reveal in her will the secret she had kept since 1957? I asked one of the partners in my firm who specialized in estate work. She said heirs who are not mentioned in a will can claim they were inadvertently omitted and may have rights that heirs who are expressly disinherited or left a pittance do not. Thus the clause leaving me a dollar. I never got the dollar, but the clause resulted in my being found.

I soon received my adoption file and learned that my legal name was Scott Francis until my adoption was finalized. So far as I know, Mama and Daddy never knew that was my name. I wonder if I would be different if it still were. And what if Julie had kept me? How would she have been different? According to the file, Julie signed the papers surrendering me when I was eight days old. Why did she wait so long? Was eight days normal? Did she struggle with the decision? Did she even make the decision? Or was it made for her? She was only 18.

When Mama and Daddy came to Jackson to see Ann Lowrey, Cliff, and Paul immediately after they were born, I noticed that Daddy was reluctant to hold them, as if they were too tiny and fragile for him to be trusted with them. The adoption file indicates that I was placed with Mama and Daddy on September 19, 1957. I was two and a half months old by then and weighed more than 11 pounds, half again as much as when I was born. Presumably they got Margie when she was a similar age. Daddy may have been reluctant to hold his newborn grandchildren because he had never held his newborn children.

The confidential report of the Louisiana Department of Welfare in the adoption file noted that Julie had brown hair, greenish-blue eyes, and an olive complexion. I have all three. The report also contained a social worker's summaries from her visits to Tupelo during my first year, before my adoption was finalized, when Mama and Daddy were being evaluated to determine if they would get to keep me. On one visit she described me as a "husky child" and declared that I "jabbered constantly." She was perceptive. When I was in Troop 12 more than a decade later, one of the older boys gave me a nickname—Babbling Brooks. Fortunately it didn't stick, but not because it didn't fit. Going through old papers, I found a letter to me from my fifth grade teacher Martha Cheney, one of the best teachers I ever had. It was dated August 1968, when I was about to start the sixth grade and a month after I became a Boy Scout. She wrote, generously, that teaching me the year before had been a pleasure and a challenge. I'm sure I was jabbering then too. It's now been more than 50 years since Mrs. Cheney taught me and I became a Scout and more than 60 since the social worker came to Rogers Drive, but I still think I have a lot to say. I love telling stories—my children say I tell the same ones over and over—and I'm still husky as well.

The file also revealed that Mama and Daddy returned to New Orleans when I was just over a year old and appeared before the Juvenile Court on July 28, 1958, to finalize the adoption. The record includes Daddy's testimony that his current annual salary was $6600. He had no reason to ask for a prenuptial agreement when he got married eight years earlier; neither did the preacher's daughter who married him. At the end of the short hearing the judge approved the adoption. On that day I ceased to be Scott Francis and became Paul Brooks Eason. I got a new name just as Ada Brooks did five decades later.

The day after I received the adoption file, Ben called. He had Lewis Bettman in St. Louis on the phone with him. Ben had

159

called Lewis because he was the executor of Julie's will. Lewis told us he had met Julie when they were in college at Washington University and they had been friends the rest of her life. He was also her financial advisor and stockbroker. Lewis told us about Julie's beauty, intelligence, and sense of humor and also about her long, losing fight with alcoholism. Before the call ended, he said he thought he knew who my father was, that he knew who was dating Julie in the fall of 1956 before she dropped out of school for the spring semester. He asked if I wanted to know. Though I had never looked for either of my birth parents and never would have, this was different. I said I would think about it.

A day or two later I spoke to Edith Morris in New Orleans. She said she was a domestic relations lawyer and was always fighting over child custody, visitation, alimony, and the like. My case was unlike anything she had ever handled. She said she and her staff were thrilled that I had been found, that I was a lawyer, and that I lived less than 200 miles away. When I said I thought I understood, she responded that she wasn't sure I did. To emphasize her point, she said that everyone in her office loved me.

Edith also said she'd just been in Juvenile Court on another matter before Judge Anita Ganucheau, the judge who'd first ordered the officials to turn over the adoption records. During a break Edith approached the judge and whispered, "We found him." Judge Ganucheau immediately called a recess and asked Edith to come back into her chambers. After Edith told the judge about me, the two of them called the judge presiding over the case in Oklahoma and told her.

One morning the following week, not long after Ben filed the pleading in Oklahoma disclosing that I was Baby Boy Francis, my office phone rang. I looked down at the number on caller ID and saw 918. I recognized that as the area code for Tulsa because Ben and I had been talking frequently. I assumed he was calling again and answered the phone by saying his name. The voice on the other end said, "No, this is Sid Smith." "Uncle Sid," I responded. "I guess so," he said.

Though it appeared that Sid and I would be on opposite sides of the lawsuit in Oklahoma fighting over the trust and the oil wells, we had a very pleasant talk. He told me he had five children—my biological first cousins—including one who was a lawyer in Hawaii, and he talked about Julie. Sid is closer to my age than to hers. She was nearly 11 when he was born and he was barely eight when I was born. He said she was beautiful and asked if I wanted to see pictures. I said absolutely and he promised to select a few, have copies made, and send them to me.

A few days later a FEDEX package from Sid arrived at my office. To that point in my nearly 47 years I'd never seen a picture of anyone related to me by blood other than my three children. I pulled out the pictures one at a time and studied them. There was one of Betty by herself, one of Julie when she was about three years old sitting in her father's lap, and another one taken a few years later of Julie surrounded by four of her cousins, all girls. After studying the first three photos in detail, I pulled out the fourth one, the first one of Julie as an adult. She looked to be in her twenties. The resemblance was remarkable. She was younger and more attractive than I was, but otherwise she looked like me with a wig. I left my office, walked down the hall, and showed the picture to my friends at the firm.

When I returned to my desk, I called Sid to thank him. In the only allusion by either of us to the trust dispute, I told him they weren't going to need a DNA test to confirm that Julie was my mother. I asked if he was sitting at a computer. When he said he was, I suggested he go to the Brunini firm's website and look up my picture. He did and agreed there was no doubt.

Soon after I received the photos from Sid, Ben sent me the court file from the proceedings involving Julie's estate in the late 1980s. The file included documents about Julie's oil and gas interests as well as her investment file and extensive stock portfolio managed by Lewis Bettman. Among the documents in the investment file were not only account statements but also correspondence from Julie, including a number of personal notes she had written to Lewis. Julie had beautiful handwriting, far better than mine, and the notes reflected her intelligence and love for travel as well as her wit and kindness. They made me think I would have liked her even if she were not my mother.

In April of 1978, as I was finishing my junior year at Ole Miss, Julie wrote Lewis's firm from Aspen to authorize him to handle all transactions in her account "in the event that I should be bounding about the world and totally unreachable by modern methods." Three years later, after her second divorce and while I was in law school in Durham, she sent Lewis $20,000 from Tulsa to be deposited into her account. On a note card labeled "The Early Pig Gets All The Truffles," she wrote, "If you could double this, we could all go to Europe for a week." When she sent another check to deposit, she reported on a "perilous journey over dead bodies: not two but three mice" on her way to mail the check. When she sent a third check "to fatten account," she promised to send Lewis a postcard of the snow-capped Colorado peaks. In November 1981, when Lewis sent roses to Julie for her 43rd birthday, she responded with a note thanking him for remembering her birthday in such an elegant manner. She later wrote him the note thanking him "for the zillionth time" for his help in her efforts to lick her "damn problem."

My favorite of Julie's notes was about a different problem. In the late 1970s a clerk at Stix & Company, the brokerage firm in St. Louis where Lewis worked, hatched a scheme in which he and several co-conspirators embezzled more than $15 million, which led to the firm's bankruptcy and ultimately its liquidation. In the course of the investigation, the government threatened to freeze the firm's client accounts, including Julie's, and ultimately did so. She had every right to be angry, but her correspondence reveals that she was less concerned about herself than about Lewis. Shortly before Christmas, in a note to his wife Gini expressing concern about him, Julie made a request: "Please don't let Lewis get angry with himself for what has happened at Stix. I hold him in no way responsible. We shall all eat and have a Merry Christmas despite the thief and the Feds who might freeze our $."

In the midst of writing this book, I learned I was a victim of a Ponzi scheme. I had invested in a fund that loaned money to a man who claimed he used it to finance the purchase of timber rights, but it turned out there was no timber and there were no rights. The man who ran the scheme, who is now serving 20 years in federal prison, forged all the documents. In classic Ponzi fashion, the money he raised from later investors was used to pay off earlier ones, not to buy trees. The discovery of the scam and the uncertainty about the extent of my loss left me in a state of depression. But then I reread Julie's kind note to Gini Bettman and her reminder that we shall all eat and have a Merry Christmas. It was as if Julie was giving me advice from the grave.

There were only a few notes in the file, but they were enough to make me feel that I knew Julie at least a little. And they made me wish I could have known her more.

Chapter 37

The end of the story—or at least the part about the trust dispute—was anticlimactic. Ben called one day with bad news. The Oklahoma Supreme Court had just decided a case that had grave implications for our case. He sent me the court's opinion and asked me to read it. The gist of the ruling was this: If a trust is supposed to terminate on the occurrence of an event and the event has already occurred but the trust was not formally terminated, then the assets are treated as if they are no longer in the trust. The trust for Julie was supposed to terminate when she turned 40, seven years before she died, which was when the final third of the principal was to be distributed to her. Based on the ruling Ben sent me, it thus appeared that the trust assets were properly treated as if Julie owned them outright. If that were the case, they correctly went to the Buell brothers under her will, and Sid and his family legally owned them now.

We could have argued that my case was different because Julie signed the trust indenture in 1973 and chose to leave the assets in the trust, but it would have been difficult to prevail. And I was not interested in pursuing a claim to the trust assets that was no better than a long shot, especially because Julie didn't intend for me to receive them and Sidney may not have ever known I existed. Ben and I could have tried to negotiate a modest settlement, but we decided not to. Just weeks after learning that I might have a valid claim to a sizable fortune, I decided to drop it.

So I didn't get rich, but I got quite a story, a story I've learned much more about while writing it. And it's almost certainly a story

I still wouldn't know if the Oklahoma Supreme Court had decided the unfavorable case several years earlier, before Ben went to all the effort to identify and find me. Had it been decided sooner, he probably wouldn't have made the effort. Instead he would have analyzed the opinion in the case and informed the judge in Tulsa that Baby Boy Francis did not have a valid claim. Then the judge would have read the opinion too, directed Ben to call off the search, and I never would have learned about Julie and her family—my second family—and the story of my birth.

And in truth, learning the story was probably far better for me than getting the assets in the trust would have been. If the dispute had been resolved in my favor, I would have received the interests in the oil wells when I was the same age Julie was when she died. Ben and I never got to the point of finding out exactly how much the trust was worth, but the amount may well have been enough for me to retire. And though it's impossible to know, having the freedom to do nothing may have been as bad for me as it was for Julie.

Chapter 38

After the initial excitement of learning the story, time passed, I got busy at work, and life resumed. From time to time I would tell the story and I occasionally considered doing something about it—searching for my birth father, going to Tulsa to meet Julie's family, even writing a book. But I was already writing another book, the one about my hiking trips with Bobby, and I also had other things on my mind.

In August 2004 Ann Lowrey and Ada Brooks headed north to Oxford and we no longer had a beautiful baby in the house. My life returned to normal, but I wasn't satisfied with it. Maybe it was a mid-life crisis, but I wasn't happy with my law firm or my marriage. Over the next several years I changed law firms twice and got a divorce.

I had been at the Brunini firm for more than two decades and had close friends there. The firm was like family to me. I had been very involved in management, serving on the firm's board of directors and chairing one of its litigation departments. But the firm had changed and I needed a change. In May 2005 I joined the Jackson office of McGlinchey Stafford, a firm based in New Orleans. The decision to leave the only firm where I'd ever worked was an emotional one and I wondered if I'd done the right thing when Hurricane Katrina flooded the city where my new firm's largest office was located only three months later.

New Orleans and McGlinchey recovered from the storm and I enjoyed my time at the firm, but I stayed less than two years. Baker Donelson, a larger firm with a much larger office in Jackson, recruited a group of us from McGlinchey beginning in early 2006. I couldn't make the move at the time because of a very large case involving a failed merger. It was the case in which I was taking depositions in St. Louis the week I toured Washington University and found out Ann Lowrey was pregnant. It was still pending in 2006, I represented the plaintiff, and lawyers at Baker Donelson did work on other matters for the defendant. If I changed firms, I would have to give up the case and I was not willing to do that. I enjoyed working on it, had become close to the New York lawyers working on it with me, and also felt an obligation not to walk out on my client. Jerry Johnson, a good friend who had recruited me to join McGlinchey a year earlier, felt awful that he was now leaving but I had to stay behind. I told him not to worry, that he could be the guinea pig. When my case ended, if he could convince me that moving to Baker Donelson was a wise decision, I would join him there.

That's ultimately what I did. After the merger case was resolved, five others from McGlinchey changed firms with me: my secretary, two associates, and two paralegals, one of whom was Ann Lowrey. She's now an educator and mother of four, but I'm still at Baker Donelson. I suppose three jobs in more than 35 years is fewer than most people have.

I had also become increasingly unhappy with my marriage. I'm sure Betsy Ann felt the same way. We had grown apart and our children were now old enough that I no longer felt the need to stay together for their benefit. I moved out over Thanksgiving in 2007 and spent the next year living alone in our cabin north of Jackson. Betsy Ann kept our two dogs and I got two cats to keep me company and rid the cabin of mice. Our divorce was finalized in December 2008.

Momie and Daddy Cliff had four children and 10 children, all of whom got married and had children of their own. Starting with Momie and Daddy Cliff's, there were 15 marriages in the three generations. Mine was the first to end in divorce.

The end of my marriage to Betsy Ann, like the end of Julie's to Lee Farnham nearly 40 years earlier, was as amicable as possible.

Betsy Ann called me the day our divorce was finalized to remind me that I had a doctor's appointment, she came to the wedding reception when I married Carrie two years later, and she often spends holidays with us. She and I share three children and four grandchildren, so it's good that we get along. Many divorced couples don't.

Chapter 39

When Betsy Ann and I separated in late 2007, she didn't want me to tell Daddy, the only one of our four parents who was still alive. She didn't want to upset him and was afraid he would have a hard time dealing with it. I disagreed—by then he had lived through a depression, a world war, and the deaths of his parents, wife, and two sisters—but I dreaded the conversation. I also had an excuse for procrastinating. Betsy Ann and I had not yet made a final decision to get a divorce, so I kept quiet. Over the course of the next year she and I traveled together to Tupelo several times to see Daddy and pretended that nothing had changed.

Near the end of 2008, on a Friday in November, I drove up for the weekend by myself. The occasion was Troop 12's 700th consecutive monthly campout. Daddy had just turned 87. He was no longer attending meetings and had gotten too old to camp by then, but I took him to the site where the troop was camping. Walking with a cane, he toured the campground and greeted the Scouts and the new generation of leaders. The younger boys in the troop didn't recognize him, but they'd been told.

Beginning Scouts are required to learn about the history of Scouting and on the campout a new one was asked to identify the Father of the Boy Scouts. The correct answer was Lord Robert Baden-Powell, who founded the Scouting movement in England in 1908 with the publication of the first installment of his *Scouting for Boys*. Exactly a century later, and more than half a century after Troop 12 started camping every month, the troop's newest member identified someone else. When asked to name the Father of the Boy Scouts, he said Paul Eason.

Betsy Ann and I took one more trip together to Tupelo in early 2009, shortly after our divorce was finalized, but then she stopped going with me. For the next two years my trips to Tupelo were either alone or with one or more of my children and grandchildren. It was a treat to watch my grandkids explore the same creek I had explored 50 years earlier and see Daddy push them in the swing hanging from an oak tree in the vacant lot. But I still didn't break the news to him. Even after Carrie and I got engaged in September 2010 and then married on New Year's Day in 2011, I kept the secret.

But in the summer of 2011 I decided enough was enough. Carrie and I had been married six months and she'd never met Daddy. As things stood, I couldn't take her to see him and I couldn't bring him to our house to see her. Both limitations were no longer acceptable. Daddy's health was also an issue. He was nearing his 90th birthday and declining, both physically and mentally. It was clear he would not be able to live alone much longer. I knew it would be a struggle to persuade him to move out of the house where he'd lived for 55 years and I needed to begin talking to him about it. He and I also needed to decide where he would go. By this point Betsy Ann had also remarried. I told her my plans and then drove alone to Tupelo for the conversation I had long dreaded.

On the way I rehearsed what I planned to say a dozen times. Daddy and I followed his standard Saturday night routine, cooking on the grill and then watching TV, a ritual that had begun with burgers and *Gunsmoke* 50 years earlier. At nine o'clock, after one show ended but before another one could begin, I hit the off button on the remote and pulled a stool up in front of Daddy's chair. He looked at me and waited. He was good at waiting.

I began by saying I was sure he'd wondered why Betsy Ann had stopped coming with me when I came to see him. That seemed like a good way to start, but from the look on his face I could see that he hadn't wondered at all. I took a deep breath and continued. I told him the divorce was amicable, explained why we hadn't told him, and said that Betsy Ann and I were both happy. I said Carrie was wonderful, my grandchildren loved her, and his nephew Eason Leake was the chairman of the board of the bank where she worked. I told him Betsy Ann's new husband was a fraternity brother of ours and had roomed at Ole Miss with another of his nephews, Phil Ruff. I spoke for ten minutes; he neither interrupted nor changed expression. When I got to the end of my spiel, he still said nothing. I asked if I could bring Carrie to Tupelo to meet him and he said that would be fine. A few seconds passed in silence, then he reached for the remote and turned the TV back on. He never once asked me why my marriage of 29 years had ended. Not then, not ever.

Two weeks later Carrie and I took the grandchildren—there were just three then—back to Tupelo. Daddy was glad to meet Carrie, she was thrilled to meet him after all I'd told her, and I kicked myself for not telling him sooner. We had a nice weekend, but it was becoming clearer than ever that Daddy could not live alone. We needed to decide on a plan right away. I wanted to bring him home with us, but I knew he would resist and, with the back seat full of grandchildren, there was no place to put him. On the drive home Carrie and I discussed options. While we were at Ann Lowrey and Paul's dropping off the little people, my cell phone rang. It was Phil Ruff, who lived in Tupelo and did a great deal to take care of Daddy after he quit driving. While taking down the American flag, which Daddy put up every morning and took down every evening, he had fallen on his front porch and broken a bone in his foot. Fortunately he was outside and a neighbor saw him and called Phil. I had to be in federal court on the Gulf Coast the next day so Carrie made a second trip to Tupelo and brought Daddy home to our house. They had met just two days before and she wondered if he thought a crazy woman had kidnapped him.

When Carrie brought Daddy from his house to ours, we initially thought we would find an assisted living facility for him, and we visited a very nice one that was only minutes away. He was impressed, but he was concerned about the cost and wondered if he could afford it. Daddy grew up in the Depression and like many of his generation was very conservative with finances. He saved for a rainy day because he'd lived through many. Even when there was little extra, he always set some money aside, saving a dime for every dollar he made. And he never made a lot. After his career was over, Daddy said he never made any money anywhere he worked. Yet despite his modest income and the fact that he always gave generously to the First Methodist Church and other charities, he managed to accumulate significant savings by the time he retired from the private sector. And his savings continued to grow during the next quarter of a century because he spent almost nothing on himself. He'd paid off the mortgage long ago and all his furniture was more than 20 years old, as were most of his clothes. And so when he asked if he could afford the assisted living facility, I told him he could, that I'd done the math and he could afford to stay there for 36 years. In 36 years he would have been two months away from his 126th birthday.

But he never had to afford it for even one month. The facility was excellent and had beautiful grounds, but the staff assessed Daddy and decided he would need to be admitted to the Alzheimer's wing. Carrie and I toured the wing and weren't comfortable with his living there. After he had been with us two weeks and we were considering other options, Carrie said we needed to stop looking. She had decided Daddy needed to live with us, that nobody would love him as much or take care of him as well as we would. I was thinking the same thing but was reluctant to suggest it. We were newlyweds and had never discussed bringing an elderly parent into our home. I will always be grateful to Carrie for welcoming Daddy and taking care of him for the two years we had the privilege to spend with him.

We treasured our time with Daddy, but meals were a challenge. He was accustomed to eating beef, pork, and chicken at nearly every meal and Carrie doesn't eat beef, pork, or chicken at any meal. During his first week with us Carrie made an arugula salad with homemade balsamic dressing to accompany our dinner. Daddy, who was an iceberg-and-thousand-island man, frowned and stirred it with his fork. Without taking the risk of tasting it, he asked if she'd picked it out of the yard. Carrie started making two meals every night, one for him and one for us. Their diets overlapped hardly at all, but they both overlapped with mine. I sat at the end of the table with Carrie to my left and Daddy to my right. I was the husky omnivore in the middle.

Daddy had not flown a plane in nearly 60 years by the time he came to live with us. He flew crop dusters until shortly after he and Mama married, when she asked him to stop because it was dangerous. He complied, let his license lapse, and never flew again. After he gave it up, he never talked about flying, at least not to me. But when he was living with us his last two years, Daddy adopted a habit that made Carrie and me think he missed flying a great deal. When the weather was nice, we would take him outside for a very slow walk around the circle in our neighborhood. He would take a few steps with the aid of his walker, then stop and look up. He would search the sky for jet contrails and point them out to us.

We also found something in Tupelo that made us believe Daddy truly loved to fly. I never once heard Daddy talk about poetry or recite a poem, but in the bedroom on Rogers Drive where he slept for 55 years we found a framed copy of a poem called "High Flight." Daddy and the poet, John Magee, were the same age and were both pilots during World War II, though they served different countries. Magee, who was in the Royal Canadian Air Force, was killed on a training flight over England four days after Pearl Harbor. He was only 19. His short poem is about the thrill of flying.

Oh! I have slipped the surly bonds of earth,
And danced the skies on laughter-silvered wings;
Sunward I've climbed, and joined the tumbling mirth
Of sun-split clouds,—and done a hundred things
You have not dreamed of—Wheeled and soared and swung
High in the sunlit silence. Hov'ring there
I've chased the shouting wind along, and flung
My eager craft through footless halls of air...
Up, up the long, delirious, burning blue

I've topped the wind-swept heights with easy grace
Where never lark or even eagle flew—
And, while with silent lifting mind I've trod
The high untrespassed sanctity of space,
Put out my hand, and touched the face of God.

I don't know where or when Daddy got the poem or if he thought of himself as a pilot who "danced the skies" like John Magee. It makes me sad to think that Daddy gave up something he loved. But that was his way. He lived for others, not for himself. He lived to be of use.

Daddy loved it when his great-grandchildren came to our house to visit and they enjoyed spending time with him. But as time passed and his memory went from bad to worse, he would ask, "Those children sure are smart, now whose are they?" For Christmas in 2012, Daddy's last one, Carrie gave me a portrait of him sitting outside with Ada Brooks, Eason, and Collins. Elsa Gray was born four months after Daddy died. We were hoping she would be born on his birthday, but she came two days too late.

Chapter 40

Daddy turned 91 in November 2012 and his health began to deteriorate rapidly the following spring. He developed an arterial blockage in one leg and the surgery to unblock it was unsuccessful. It was only the second time he'd been hospitalized in his entire life. After the surgery he stopped eating nearly altogether. He didn't even want ice cream. His primary physician, Lee Sams, an old friend of mine who grew up in Tupelo, said we should offer him food but not force him to eat, that if we did he might live just long enough for his foot to have to be amputated. His vascular surgeon agreed. He told me he always tried to remember that the goal should be to prolong life, not prolong death.

Daddy ate little of what we offered but was still able to sit in his recliner and throw the tennis ball for Mollie to fetch. Wonderful caregivers from hospice came and told us what to expect. I drafted his obituary, which was my honor to write, and asked Lewis Whitfield of Tupelo, one of Daddy's early Eagle Scouts, if he would prepare and deliver the eulogy at Daddy's funeral. He said it would be his honor to give it.

Not long after he came to live with us, Daddy told Carrie and me we had saved his life by bringing him from Tupelo to our house. He was easy to care for and appreciated everything we did for him. Near the end, however, he became very stubborn about one thing: having to bathe. We would beg and plead and Carrie would stress the need for him to be fresh when his great-grandchildren came to visit. I was more direct. He would finally relent and I would put on a swimsuit, help him onto his chair in the shower, then get in with him and bathe him. He would complain that the water was too cold or too hot and, when I barely nudged the nob in response, that it was too hot or too cold. I reminded him that he'd spent more than a thousand nights sleeping outside in all kinds of weather, both hotter and colder than the shower.

The first day the hospice workers came, we left them there with Daddy and Chris, the sitter we'd hired to stay with him. That afternoon the hospice nurse called. She said the elderly often don't like to bathe and hospice workers are trained to deal with their objections and persuade them. They had tried everything with Daddy, but nothing had worked. He was steadfast. I told her I would stay home the next day and try to convince him.

After the orderly arrived the following morning, I stood at the foot of Daddy's bed and explained his options. The orderly could give him a sponge bath in the bed. He was trained to do it, he would use warm water, and it would take only a few minutes. Or, if Daddy still refused, the orderly and I would get him out of the bed and onto his wheelchair and roll him to the bathroom. Then we would lift him up, take off his pajamas, put him on his chair in the shower, and I would get in the shower with him. After he was clean, the orderly and I would lift him back up, dry him off, dress him, and bring him back to bed. Daddy was shaking his head the whole time I was talking. I asked him what it was going to be, if he was going to cooperate with the sponge bath. With a look of disgust he said one word: "somewhat." I walked out the door before he could change his mind.

Daddy slept almost all the last weekend of June. He died at noon on Monday, July 1, four months before his 92nd birthday and two days before my 56th. I was at work giving a presentation to the young lawyers in our firm and got two calls, first from Chris and then from Carrie. I couldn't answer either one, but I knew what they meant. When I got home, Chris told me she had been sitting beside Daddy when he stopped breathing. She said being with him when he passed away was a blessing on her soul.

Her mission complete, Chris was now out of a job. After the coroner left and the undertaker took Daddy's body, I told her I was going to the bank to get some money for a severance payment. She asked if I would do her a favor and get her something else too. Chris was deeply religious; she brought her worn Bible to our house every day and read it while Daddy watched TV. Her request surprised me. She asked me to stop at a convenience store and get her a pack of Marlboro Lights. Daddy had died and she wanted a smoke.

Daddy's funeral was a testament to a life well lived in service to others. Lewis Whitfield's eulogy was just right. Dozens of Daddy's former Scouts attended, some from far away. Lewis asked all the Eagle Scouts in the sanctuary to stand. I stood in the front row and turned around so I could see Daddy's other Eagles behind me. I kept my composure until we closed the service by singing Taps, which a bugler had played every night at Boy Scout camp when I was in Troop 12.

In the wake of Daddy's death and the publication of his obituary, I got beautiful messages from many who knew him, primarily his Scouts, about how much he'd meant to them. Some said Daddy had been the most influential man in their lives. Others said he was one of the two most influential and named their own father as the other. My favorite message was from Tupelo lawyer Mike Bush, who was not in Troop 12 but had camped often with the troop when his son was a member. After describing his fondness for the other members of Daddy's family, Mike turned to Daddy:

"It is no disparagement to your family to say that your father was a standout. He knew what was important in life. One just felt better in his presence, always. You mentioned Carrie taking him in. I do not know her, but would place a healthy wager that she was well rewarded by the relationship. I certainly was.

"When my son Marshall was in Troop 12, I did my share of camping. Your father prepared a peach cobbler toward the end of every evening, cooking it under the coals of the fire as I recall. He cooked by smell; when it smelled done, it was. Somewhere around 10 p.m., all these spoons would gather around his campfire, drawn by the smell, no faces mind you, just outreached spoons in the dark of the night, reflecting the campfire light. Magical.

"We should all be more like Paul Eason. We just do not know how."

Mike would have won his wager. Carrie will tell anyone who asks that she was very well rewarded by her relationship with Daddy. He lived with us less than two years and has been gone far longer than that, but every now and then, out of the blue, she turns to me and says, "I miss your daddy."

Chapter 41

Years after Daddy died, I learned a number of the things I've written about him from my cousin Elizabeth Leake Keckler, who was two generations younger than Daddy, never lived in the same town he did, and hardly knew him until he was over 80. That I learned them from her and not from him is proof of Daddy's reluctance to talk about himself and my failure to ask.

Elizabeth is the daughter of my cousin Eason Leake and his wife Ellen, who live in Jackson. Eason is the only child of Tut and Bob, my aunt and uncle. Years ago, in Elizabeth's last semester of high school, her English teacher assigned her to interview and write a story about a family member. Eason suggested Daddy, who was Bubba to him, and he and Elizabeth drove up the Natchez Trace to Tupelo one morning in early 2003. They spent four hours with Daddy, first in his den and then on a driving tour of the city. Years later, long after Daddy died, Eason and Ellen gave me the notes Elizabeth took that day as well as cassette tapes of their conversation. One weekend in the summer of 2018 I borrowed a cassette player and listened to Daddy's voice for the first time since his death.

The conversation I listened to took place more than three years after Mama died, but Daddy was still in great shape both physically and mentally. He had turned 81 several months earlier but was still meeting with the Scouts every week and camping with them every month. On Sundays he drove residents of an assisted living center to and from services at the First Methodist Church. He was older than many of his passengers.

From the tapes I learned about the Model T Ford Daddy bought for $25 in 1940 so he could take flying lessons to prepare for the war that was coming. I also learned that he didn't like his first job at McCarty Holman when he returned to Tupelo and applied for a position with the FBI before accepting one with Milam Manufacturing. I heard him say that Troop 12 met outside for a year not long after he became the leader because the church had no place inside for them to meet.

Daddy told Elizabeth a story about one of his early Scouts, Eugene Worley, the oldest of three brothers who all became Eagle Scouts in the troop. Eugene studied engineering at Mississippi State, went to work for NASA in Huntsville, Alabama, and came back to Tupelo one weekend in the mid-'60s to camp with the troop. Sitting by the campfire, he told Daddy of NASA's plan to put a man on the moon. Daddy thought it was pie in the sky and said, "You're crazy; nobody's ever going to the moon."That was just like Daddy, telling a story about when he was wrong. Daddy had a great deal to brag about, but I never once heard him brag. When former Scouts came back from all over the country for Troop 12's 500th and 600th consecutive monthly campouts, it never occurred to Daddy that they made the trip to see and honor him.

In the midst of the interview Daddy's orange tabby cat named Pip walked into the den. Pip had belonged to Mike and Janet Armour when they lived across the street. They moved two miles away and took Pip with them, but he liked his old neighborhood more than he liked them. He repeatedly disappeared from his new home and showed up on Rogers Drive. Daddy would return him or Mike and Janet would come get him, but he kept coming back. Finally the Armours gave up and Pip became Daddy's cat. While he was talking to Elizabeth and Eason, Daddy related something odd about the cat that I'd forgotten. Pip refused to drink water from a bowl and demanded running water. When he was thirsty, he would jump up onto the kitchen counter and sit by the sink until Daddy turned on the faucet. When he had drunk his fill, he would jump down and Daddy would turn it off.

One question Elizabeth asked Daddy that I never asked him was why he enlisted in the Navy and not the Army during the war.

He said you could sleep on a ship in the Navy, but in the Army you had to sleep on the ground. I was listening to what he said 15 years after he said it, but I wanted to interrupt. I wanted to stop him and remind him of what he did after the war, of all the campouts and all the nights he spent sleeping on the ground. And I would have pointed out that nobody made him do it.

In the file Eason and Ellen gave me was a draft of the letter Elizabeth sent Daddy in 2003 thanking him for his time and telling him how much the experience meant to her. Elizabeth suffered from juvenile diabetes in her teens and in the letter she thanked Daddy for making a gift in her honor to the Juvenile Diabetes Research Foundation. Fifteen years later, shortly before I read the draft of Elizabeth's letter, her mother Ellen was selected to serve as the chairman of the international board of the foundation.

I listened to the last of the four one-hour tapes lying in bed on Sunday night, July 1. After the tape came to an end, I told Carrie all the new things I'd learned about Daddy. Then something occurred to me that I also told her: Daddy had died five years ago to the day.

Four months after listening to the tapes, on what would have been Daddy's 97th birthday, I posted a photo of him in his Navy uniform on Facebook. The picture had been taken three quarters of a century earlier. I ended the message I wrote about him with a question: How many lives did he touch? Some whose lives he touched posted comments on Facebook in response. They included:

```
He touched too many lives to count!
No way to tell but in the many thou-
sands!! He was a quiet, hardworking hero.
He touched my life in many positive
ways. After my dad, he was the second
most influential man in my life.
He is still touching lives every day.
I am a Scoutmaster because of Eason. He
can take credit for another Eagle Scout
this week, a boy in our troop.
```

He was a major influence in my life. My four sons also became Eagle Scouts.

I have been involved with Scouting for the last 10 years. My son earned his Eagle this summer. I can still remember listening to Mr. Eason as he helped me during many a campout.

Because of Mr. Eason, I am still involved in Scouting. All I am is because of him and my father, who was also one of his Eagles.

He was an incredible man and a huge influence in my life. He told me the only way out of Scouts was to attain your Eagle. He expected great things from young men and got great things from them.

Paul was a wonderful man. He was the best Scoutmaster in the world.

Finest man I ever knew.

He helped me raise two sons.

The inspiration to "do good" that Paul Eason instilled in so many people will ripple throughout the world forever.

Four months after I posted Daddy's photo on Facebook, I posted one of Mama and wrote about her on what would have been her 98th birthday. Daddy got a great deal of praise for his work with the Boy Scouts and rightfully so, but Mama didn't get enough for the support she gave him. For nearly the entire length of their marriage, he left her at home one weekend every month to go camping with Troop 12. And it was a marriage that began in 1950 and ended when she died four months before their 50th anniversary.

In the early years Mama stayed at home alone when Daddy went camping. From the time they adopted Margie until I left for college, she was responsible for taking care of one or both of us while he was gone. For the second half of their marriage, from the time I started at Ole Miss until she died, she was again by herself on campout weekends. Some women would have complained, but not Mama. She wasn't a complainer and was content being alone. She would do chores around the house, paint, and read. I wrote on Facebook that she was smart and funny and that I missed her. Carrie often says she wished she could have known Mama. Friends in Tupelo who did know her added the following comments to my Facebook post:

I loved her so much. She used to come to the Christian Life Center at church and roller skate. She would put on her big band music and skate all over that place.

She was a treasure for Tupelo and your family.

Your mom was great! You and I had great childhoods.

You were blessed with a great mama. She was always kind and supportive. We still have her original charcoal painting of our first house here in Tupelo on Highland Circle (next to the Eason house) and we treasure it.

I have great memories of that lady.

I have great memories of our neighbors on Rogers Drive. All of you were very special. Eddie and I also got married in 1950. We will celebrate our 70th anniversary next February.

She was a great lady, Brooks. She and your father helped raise many of us growing up in Tupelo.

Margaret was a wonderful person. I loved her dearly.

Chapter 42

Among the papers we found in Daddy's house when he came to live with Carrie and me was a large manila envelope with my name on it. Inside were a number of documents from my earliest years: my feeding schedule when I was an infant; the announcement of my baptism at First Methodist Church in March 1958 when I was christened with a name that was not yet legally mine; the notice to Mama and Daddy to appear in court in New Orleans four months later to finalize my adoption; and the list of supplies I was to take to school when I started the first grade at Joyner Elementary School five years later.

Also among the documents was a scrap of paper that had been torn from an appointment calendar. There were notes on the back in Mama's handwriting. When I first saw it, I wondered why the scrap of paper got placed in the envelope with the more official documents. But then I read what Mama had written. She had recorded my date of birth and my weight when I was born, when I was a month old, and again when I was two months old. She had also written "lt. br. hair, blue eyes, Eng. Irish" and "1 sem. of college, western state, sports, dancing, cooking." I knew then when she had written the notes and why she had kept them.

Margie was two years old. Mama and Daddy wanted to adopt a second child, this time a son. Mama had repeatedly made their wishes known to Methodist Home Hospital in New Orleans, the home for unwed mothers from which they had adopted their first. There was only one explanation for the notes. Mama wrote them when she got the call with the good news, the news that there was a baby boy waiting at the home for them. She would have grabbed a pencil and the paper that was closest to the phone, the appointment calendar, and written down what the social worker told her about the baby that would soon be theirs. She would have asked about the baby's mother and recorded what she learned about her as well. Daddy was at work and she didn't want to forget anything, not that she would. She later tore her notes out of the calendar and saved them for me. When I read the notes, I first thought about the call Mama got from New Orleans and the conversation when she wrote them. Then I imagined the one that came later, when Daddy got home from work that afternoon.

Mama has changed into her prettiest dress. She waits in their tiny kitchen, then hops up to greet him when she sees the door knob turn. She hugs him harder and longer than usual, then steps back. She is glowing. Daddy is a patient man, as good Boy Scout leaders have to be. He waits to hear why.

"She called."

"She? Who's she?"

"Guess." She tugs on his sleeve.

He thinks he knows—only one thing could make her act this way—but he plays along. "Marjory. She's found a man."

"Wrong. Guess again. It was long distance. From out of state."

"I give up."

"Louisiana."

"I give up again."

"New Orleans."

"Really? A maternity home in New Orleans?"

She nods.

"Methodist Home Hospital?"

"That's the one."

"Let's go to the living room."

"Okay, let me get my notes."

Notes. Of course. The scientist took notes. He waits for her to take her spot on the couch, then sits on the side chair next to it. Both lean in, their knees touching.

"So I was just starting supper and the phone rings and I say 'hello' and the woman says, 'Mrs. Eason' and I say 'this is she' and she says, 'we have a baby boy for you.' Just like that. Those were her exact words."

"I'm sure they were."

The lab technician, precise.

"So I ask her to tell me about the baby. Our baby. He was born on July the third, Paul. The day before the Fourth of July."

"You're right about that."

She gives him a look. "And he weighed seven pounds and four ounces then and he weighs eleven pounds and three ounces now." She looks down at her notes. "His mother has light brown hair and blue eyes and her ancestors came from England and Ireland."

"Mine too."

"She said the girl likes dancing, sports, and cooking and I said me too."

"I like sports and eating." Daddy rarely cooked except on campouts and he never danced. "You said girl. How old is she?"

"She's finished one semester of college. She's 18."

"Exactly half your age."

She sticks out her tongue. "And she's from a western state."

"Which one?"

"She wouldn't tell me. And listen to this. When I asked why not, she said the girl was from a very prominent family so they have to be extra careful to keep everything a secret."

"So our baby's famous?"

"Our baby's two and a half months old, Paul."

"So when can we get him?"

"Our bags are packed. We leave first thing in the morning."

"I can't go tomorrow. We've got a shipment going out."

"I called Gartrell. He said he'd handle it. He made me promise we'd come straight to the plant for everybody to see him when we get back. Do you still want to call him Brooks?"

"Sure. One Paul in the house is enough. What about Margie? We'll need to find someone to keep her."

"I called Momie. We're dropping her off on the way out of town."

"Tomorrow? Really?"

"Tomorrow. Really."

"I can't believe I'm gonna have a son."

"*We're* gonna have a son, Paul. *We* are."

He leans forward and kisses her.

After imagining the conversation between Mama and Daddy, I thought of an earlier one, a sadder one, between the social worker and Julie, who was in the midst of surrendering her child but was little more than a child herself. According to the brochure for the home, each birth mother was promised that her baby would be placed in a "sober, substantial, Christian family" and assured that she was "adding to the sum total of the world's happiness by making it possible for a woman who could never have a child of her own to know the love and affection of a precious baby."

So the social worker would have told Julie that good parents would be found for her baby boy, parents who would love him. She could not have known how right she was. She then would have asked Julie: "Tell me some things about you. What may we tell the couple who will adopt your son about his mother? What do you like to do?" Julie would have named three things she enjoyed —sports, dancing, and cooking. Later she would have held me and looked at me for the last time. Then she would have handed me back, signed the papers, and closed that chapter of her life. At least she would have tried.

Chapter 43

Before I learned about Julie, I had thought very little about how adoption affects people. And until I was far along in the process of writing this story, I had never read a word about the psychological effects of adoption. I had not reviewed any articles or studies or read any books about the effect on any of the parties to the adoption triangle: birth mothers (and sometimes fathers), adoptive parents, and adoptees. So I decided to do some reading to give me a better understanding of the people I was writing about, including me.

One of the first articles I came across evaluated both the good and bad effects on children who are adopted. The article, which I read months after writing about my early memory of being read to by Mama on my bunk bed with the windows open, stated that adopted children are far more likely than other children to be read to by their parents. Adoptees are also more likely to be sung to and told stories, have good health and health insurance, participate in extracurricular activities, and do well in reading, language, arts, and math. They are less likely to live in families below the poverty line. These differences undoubtedly reflect the fact that adoptive parents tend to be stable and mature, prepared to have a family, and able to provide for one. And unlike many birth parents, they want a child, often desperately.

These differences are based on a comparison of adoptees to all other children. The differences would unquestionably be even greater if the comparison were limited to adoptees and children who are kept and raised by single mothers. Single mothers are often young and poor, their pregnancies unplanned and unwanted. Many are unprepared both emotionally and financially for the responsibilities of parenthood and rightly conclude that stable couples with resources will be more likely to give their children a good life.

Birth mothers choose to give up their babies for a host of reasons, nearly all of them unselfish. Among the reasons they cite are so their children can grow up in safe and stable homes with two parents. Birth mothers want their children to have families that are financially secure, spend time together, have close relationships with extended family members, and provide their children with opportunities to travel and pursue higher education. I had all of that and more.

That is not to say there are no negative effects associated with adoption. One study found that adopted children are more than twice as likely as others to be treated in outpatient mental clinics and more than five times as likely to be admitted to residential psychiatric facilities. They're also far more likely to develop substance abuse problems as adults. Among the causes of their problems are low self-esteem, identity issues, including uncertainty about where they fit in, difficulty forming emotional attachments, and a sense of grief and loss related to their birth families. I've gone through low points in my life, but I don't believe that being adopted had anything to do with any of them. Mama and Daddy always made me feel secure. I was their son. That I was adopted was an interesting but inconsequential detail. And I assumed my birth mother had good reasons for not being able to keep me. I was curious about her but felt no grief, no anger, and no sense of loss. I never once felt I had been abandoned.

I believe the biggest challenge I faced in being the son of Paul and Margaret Eason was not that I was adopted but that they were so good. Mama was as good as gold, a committed wife and wonderful mother. She supported Daddy and his extraordinary commitment to the Boy Scouts without complaint, at least not one that I ever heard, for the entire duration of their marriage of nearly 50 years. She was very bright and well-read and excelled at crossword puzzles. She was also wise and thoughtful and had a wonderful sense of humor. She loved to dress up at Halloween, put on a mask, get down on her knees, and trick the neighbors into thinking she was a child wanting candy. Mama was also very active in the church and totally devoted to Daddy, Margie, and me. Her only vice, smoking, was one she became addicted to long before it was considered a vice.

And then there was Daddy, who had no vices at all and was revered by all who knew him, and with good reason. Having a father who always does the right thing can be difficult for an only son who often doesn't. I wanted to measure up, but I never did. I still don't.

I don't mean to suggest that Daddy was perfect. He rarely displayed his emotions and had a hard time showing affection, a trait he shared with Daddy Cliff. He and I always shook hands; we never hugged. So did he and Daddy Cliff. It was not their way to hug another man, even their only sons. And, in spite of all the time he spent in nature, Daddy didn't show his love for it like I do. I believe there was poetry in Daddy's soul—after all, he kept a poem about the joy of flying—but like many of his generation, he kept his light under a bushel.

In 1991, two months before he turned 70, Daddy and I rafted the entire length of the Grand Canyon, a magnificent week-long trip through one of the marvels of the natural world. We rode the rapids, gazed at the amazing canyon walls, and hiked up creeks during the day. At night we slept under the stars, never putting up a tent. With no humidity and far from city lights, the night sky was amazing. We would lie in our sleeping bags and count the shooting stars. It was unlike anything those who spend their nights in cities ever see.

Before the trip Daddy decided he would keep a journal. Each afternoon after we made camp, I would see him perched on a rock writing. I didn't question him about it while we were on the river, but on the flight home I asked to read what he'd written.

I don't know what I expected, but I expected more. There was little about the beauty of the mile-high canyon that has been carved by the river over many millions of years and no description of all the colors of the canyon walls or how they change as the sun goes

down over the rim and day turns to night. There was nothing at
all about the night sky, the bright swath of the Milky Way, or the
shooting stars. We had rafted through one of the most magnificent
places on Earth, but Daddy's journal was almost entirely about our
meals. He listed everything we were served at each one, including
appetizers, entrees, side dishes, and condiments. He was not content
to say we had sandwiches when we stopped on a sandbar for lunch.
Instead it was cold cuts, tomatoes, lettuce, olives, and cheeses. There
was far more detail about what we ate than what we saw and not
a word about how what we saw made him feel.

When Daddy gave a speech ten years later at the banquet at
Troop 12's 600th campout, it was similar. He focused entirely on
facts and figures about the history of the troop. He said nothing
about the magic of a campfire, much less the reflection of the fire-
light on spoons held by boys who became better men as a result of
the years they spent in Troop 12.

But Daddy's flaws, if they can be called flaws, were the result of
his being a private man, reluctant to reveal his deepest thoughts
and more comfortable writing about food than feelings. He was
like many men of his generation and it's not fair to judge any man
without considering the times in which he lived. If Daddy had
been born in a different time, he might have been a different man.
And his shortcomings, such as they were, were not failings in how
he treated people. They were not ethical or moral. I knew Daddy
almost 56 years and never saw him do a single thing that was dis-
honest, cruel, or selfish. Not one. We tend to regard famous people
as great, but mostly they're just famous. Daddy was a great man.

Chapter 44

Research shows that adoption can also have adverse effects on adoptive parents. That seems counterintuitive; after all, the parents are now getting exactly what they've longed for: a child. But the child they're adopting is often not the child they truly want. The decision to adopt often follows the discovery that the couple cannot have children of their own. Adoption becomes the only option, the last resort. Infertility causes grief and pain and often leads to feelings of inadequacy, depression, and envy. Mama and Daddy were 28 when they got married in 1950, Mama nearly 29. They were much older than the norm in the post-war years. Two of Daddy's younger sisters were already married. One had a son; the other soon would. Mama and Daddy probably began trying to conceive a child not long after their wedding, but they were unsuccessful. Daddy was his parents' only son. It must have pained him greatly when he learned he couldn't have a son of his own.

Adoptive parents may have additional problems after the adoption is complete. Some suffer from a condition that is common enough that it has a name, Post-Adoption Depression Syndrome or PADS. The symptoms are similar to those of postpartum depression and include loss of interest in activities, difficulty concentrating, fatigue, and irritability. Adoptive parents may also have difficulty bonding with children who are not their own flesh and blood. They may question whether they're entitled to parent children they've adopted and whether they have the right to discipline them.

None of this is to say that adoption should be prohibited or even discouraged. Not surprisingly I strongly support adoption and believe it's often the best choice for everyone. The birth mother who is not ready or able to raise a child has the comfort of knowing that her baby will be placed with a couple who are, the adoptive parents get to raise a child even though they're unable to have one of their own, and the child is brought up in a home that's stable and secure. But even when it's the best choice for all three, it is not without complications for all of them.

Some adoptive parents experience none of the problems others do, or at least don't seem to. Jackson lawyer Tommy Louis is a close friend of mine. He and his best friend Roy Liddell and I have hiked and camped together in Canada and throughout the West. Tommy is a passionate man, passionate about hiking, biking, and music, about his dog Floyd, and about his wife Addie and their only child Lucie. Moderation is not his strong suit.

Like Mama and Daddy, Tommy was almost 30 when he and Addie got married. When they tried to start a family and she didn't get pregnant, they decided they wanted to adopt, but they found that the number of available babies was limited. The prevalence of abortion after *Roe v. Wade* and the societal acceptance of unwed mothers' keeping their children had combined to reduce the supply to a level far below the demand. There are now more than 30 couples trying to adopt for each child given up for adoption. In the hope that they would be one of the fortunate couples, Tommy and Addie found a woman who specialized in finding and placing babies for adoption and asked her to help. They got their hopes up several times only to be disappointed. In one case the birth mother changed her mind after seeing her baby for the first time.

When the woman called about yet another possibility, Tommy and Addie decided not to get their hopes up again. They did nothing to prepare the nursery. They bought no diapers, no formula, no baby clothes. They went about their business as if the woman had never called. But then one day she called again. She was in her car driving to Jackson and was bringing the baby with her. She was only an hour away. Panicked calls were made and relatives rushed to the grocery store and bought what Tommy and Addie had not bought. They arrived at the Louises' home just before the newest Louis got there.

Tommy, who was on the eve of his 40th birthday when he became a father, has doted on Lucie from day one. Perhaps because he was older than most new fathers and had wanted a child for so long, and perhaps because an adopted child is the most precious of gifts, he did something remarkable. Every single night of the first year of Lucie's life, Tommy wrote his new daughter a short letter. Even when he was lying in a tent in the Cascade Mountains in Washington on a hiking trip, with his headlamp as the only source of light, he wrote her a letter.

My adoption file says Mama and Daddy were selected to be my parents in part because the staff at Methodist Home Hospital thought I would look like Daddy, whom they had met two years earlier when he and Mama adopted Margie. I look very little like Daddy, but I will always be grateful that the staff thought I would. Lucie's now all grown up. She's tall, blonde, and fair. Tommy and Addie are none of the above. Tommy's less than five and a half feet tall and his family came from Lebanon. When he grows a goatee on our hiking trips, he looks just like Al Pacino. If the prospect of physical similarity had been a consideration in Lucie's case, she would not be Lucie Louis.

Tommy, Roy, and I grilled burgers on a Sunday night in the summer of 2018 to plan another hiking trip. Lucie had graduated from high school two months before—she was one of the Jackson Prep graduates to whom Jonny Drake gave the commencement address—and was leaving for college in only three weeks. Tommy was worried about how he would deal with her being gone and told us about the letters he'd written her 18 years before. He'd never told her about them or given them to her, but he had kept them and planned to have them bound into a book. He said he would give them to her on a special occasion, perhaps her wedding day. I suggested a different occasion—that he present her with the letters written by a new father on the day she becomes a new mother. Maybe Lucie will give birth to a baby that day, but maybe she'll become a mother the way her mother and my mother did. Addie is no less Lucie's mother and Mama no less mine because they didn't give birth to us.

To the best of my knowledge Mama and Daddy, like Tommy and Addie, experienced none of the problems that some adoptive parents experience. When I learned that adoptive parents may question their right to discipline their children, I thought back to my childhood and the times I wished Mama and Daddy had questioned their right to discipline me. I got many spankings, all richly deserved. They did not believe in sparing the rod or spoiling the child and did neither. Mama once broke a cedar paddle on my backside.

But maybe they were more troubled than I realized when they learned they could not have children of their own and would have to turn to adoption as their only way to have a family, though I don't believe so. In the long letter Mama wrote me in December 1985 but never put in the mail, she described me as "chosen" and declared, "Believe me, psychiatrists and psychologists say it is a proven fact that adopted children are loved more than birth children. Just giving birth doesn't make one a mother or father, except through the physical aspect. Paul and I agree with the psychiatrists and psychologists." I don't know if it's true that adopted children are loved more than birth children, but I know Mama and Daddy loved me.

Chapter 45

Much has been written about the effect on birth mothers of giving up their children for adoption during the era when Julie gave me up. Considering what a typical birth mother went through, it is not surprising that the negative consequences were often significant and long-lasting.

The pain began when the birth mother learned she was pregnant. The pregnancy was unplanned; she was not married and not ready to be a mother. She had other plans and the pregnancy interrupted them. She was often forced to leave a job, drop out of school, or move away from home. The stress of the pregnancy and the decisions she faced may have brought an end to her relationship with the baby's father as happened in Ann Lowrey's case. The mother's relationships with her family and friends may have suffered as well. Her parents may have been angry, embarrassed, and unsympathetic.

At some point the decision not to keep the child was made. She may have gone along with it only because of pressure from her parents, the baby's father, his parents, or all of them. She struggled with what to do and had second thoughts, then third, especially when the day came and she saw and held her baby for the first time. Adoption may have been the best choice, the obvious choice, but this was her baby. Who would love this baby more than she would?

All the while she was dealing with the effects pregnancy has on all women, suffering through morning sickness, watching as her belly swelled, perhaps her feet too. At some point she felt the baby move and kick for the first time, proof that another life was growing inside her. At the end of nine months she went into labor and, after hours of pain, pushed her baby out into the world. The doctor announced it was a boy and then handed this greatest of all miracles to her. The baby, who had started out smaller than the head of a pin, now weighed eight pounds and had his grandmother's nose and his father's eyes. She gave him a name. She held him close and kissed him, fed him, and listened to the noises he made.

But not for long. The nurse came into the room and said it was time. The new mother held her baby one last time. Then she handed him to the nurse, never to see him again. She gathered her things, left the maternity home, and went back to life as it was before. But it was not the same. For some birth mothers it never would be.

In *On Death and Dying* Elizabeth Kübler-Ross compared the effect of giving up a baby to the death of a family member. Both result in profound feelings of grief and loss, but in some ways giving up a baby may take a greater emotional toll. After an adoption there is no public acknowledgement of the loss, nothing akin to a funeral, and in most cases the birth mother knows nothing about her child's life after the adoption. She remains in the dark, wondering. For that reason others have likened giving up a baby to having a family member who is missing, whose fate is unknown. There is no closure.

Counseling for birth mothers is rarely adequate. When I was born in the 1950s, it was almost non-existent. There was often little sympathy for birth mothers. To the contrary, their pregnancies were regarded as a matter of shame for them and their families. Instead of the love and support a scared pregnant girl needs, there were guilt, secrecy, and silence. After the baby came, the pregnancy and birth were treated as an unpleasant episode to be swept under the rug and forgotten. Persons dealing with grief caused by a profound loss need to be able to confide in others who understand their pain. Most birth mothers did just the opposite. They didn't talk to family and friends, and they didn't seek out other birth mothers. Having a baby out of wedlock was like being gay. It was to be kept in the closet. As one birth mother put it, "It was never to be mentioned, it was never to be grieved, it was just to be denied."

A birth mother often mourned not only the loss of her child

but also the loss of her opportunity to be a mother. She worried about her child and imagined what he or she had become and would become. She thought about the adoptive parents and wondered who and where they were and how they treated the baby she had carried for nine months and then surrendered. Thoughts of the child returned on milestones in the life she was missing—the child's birthdays, when he or she would be learning to walk and talk, starting school, learning to drive. If she had other children that she kept and raised, she thought about her missing child on milestones in their lives too. She often went through the five stages of grief: denial, anger, bargaining, depression, and acceptance. But the final stage meant accepting the loss as part of her life, not eliminating it. Some birth mothers report that they had a sense of loss that was all-encompassing. They had difficulty making peace with their pasts and struggled for many years.

In *The Girls Who Went Away: The Hidden History of Women Who Surrendered Children for Adoption in the Decades Before Roe v. Wade*, author Ann Fessler documented her findings from interviews with more than a hundred birth mothers who were sent to maternity homes during the years between the end of World War II and 1973, when *Roe v. Wade* was decided, years that encompassed the Baby Boom but also came to be known as the Baby Scoop Era. The book is a powerful and heartbreaking story of how pregnant girls and young women were treated as well as the effect the ordeal had on them.

Most of the women Fessler spoke to were teenagers when they got pregnant, often in high school. Some became pregnant the very first time they had sex. Others had only a vague understanding of the connection between sex and pregnancy. But whatever the circumstances, when two teenagers fell in love and the girl got pregnant, it was treated as her fault, not his. Society considered her the culpable one, the one who should have set limits. After all, boys will be boys. And the consequences, like the blame, fell almost entirely on the girl. Most high schools and colleges barred pregnant girls from attending classes, so it was the girl and not her boyfriend who had to drop out. And it was also the girl whose reputation was destroyed. She was in love, she'd never had sex with anyone else, and yet she was now viewed as a slut and a whore, often by members of her own family. What is the male synonym for slut? There's not one, at least not one as denigrating. Playboy? Lothario? Skirt chaser? They don't quite measure up.

A boy's parents, instead of acknowledging that the girl didn't get pregnant all by herself and that their son may well have pushed her into having sex, often reacted by defending him and attacking her. Some accused her of trying to trap him and force him to marry her, and others questioned whether the baby was his. Some did both.

A girl's own parents were often no kinder. Even when they had done nothing to explain the facts of life to their teenage daughter, some reacted to news of the pregnancy with anger and disgust. They often refused to do anything to help their daughter keep and raise her baby. That would have been condoning her immoral behavior. One woman Fessler interviewed said her parents made the consequences she would face if she kept her baby clear: "Don't come home again if you plan to keep that child. We're not going to help you."

Parents feared being ostracized by their friends and neighbors and reacted by ostracizing their daughters. And so their daughters became the girls who went away. They were taken to maternity homes and left there, abandoned and afraid, to await the birth and the inevitable act that followed—giving up the baby to be raised by strangers.

But for some girls their time in the home was the least painful phase of the entire ordeal. They were surrounded by others in the same predicament, other girls their age who'd also fallen in love and also failed to set limits. Though society may have judged the girls, they didn't judge each other. But they were separated from family and friends and many felt isolated. In some homes they were not free to come and go and felt like they were in prison.

The homes also did a very poor job preparing the girls for the inevitable pain that comes with carrying a baby for nine months, giving birth, and then giving the baby away. Birth mothers needed to talk about the pain they felt and would feel, work through the shame and the grief, but that was not the way it was done. Professional counselors thought the best approach was for girls to put what happened out of their minds and get on with their lives, to think of the procedure at the end of their pregnancies as little more than an appendectomy. One young woman sobbed at the thought of giving up her newborn son and was told by a nun from the maternity home, "You know what? You're gonna forget all about this, you're gonna go home and meet a nice young man, and you're gonna get married, and you're gonna have other babies, and you're gonna forget you ever had this one." Another new mother was told, "This experience will end. You will forget that you were here. You will forget that you went through this. It will all be in the past. Given time, it will fade. You will get over it."

The counselors had good intentions, but they were wrong. A baby is not an appendix and the birth mothers couldn't put the experience out of their minds. They didn't forget and many didn't get over it. Fessler wrote that the women she interviewed frequently described the surrender of their child as the most significant and defining event of their lives. One birth mother told Fessler that "any woman who's had a child knows the depth of feeling she has for that child, and can imagine the pain you would go through if you lost that child. To not even be allowed to look at your child, to feel it inside of you and then have it gone into thin air—it leaves you feeling like a shell." No matter what they were told, most birth mothers couldn't just move on. To the contrary, as the same woman said, "that baby is with them every breath they take, every second of their lives. Every prayer, that baby is with them forever." Another woman told Fessler that she was "conscious every single day that there is a little person out there... Is he happy? Did I do the right thing? I must have done the right thing. Everybody said I was doing the right thing."

Not surprisingly, the entire experience—being sent away and shunned, having a baby, and immediately giving the baby up—scarred many birth mothers with serious psychological problems. They often suffered from a host of symptoms, including depression, persistent guilt and shame, self-loathing, an enduring sense of emptiness and loss, chronic loneliness and sadness, inability to trust, and difficulty with intimacy and maintaining relationships. One woman told Fessler she felt she was worthless, beyond redemption, and deserved nothing. Another said that "when you give up your baby, you don't feel you deserve much of anything, let alone happiness."

Many women dealt with the pain of giving up a child by turning to substance abuse. Fessler found that some women spent years self-medicating with drugs and alcohol. When one returned to school after giving up her baby, she just wanted to escape. She smoked pot and drank for 15 years and couldn't hold a job. She cared about nothing. Another said she went away to college and started drinking to numb the pain. "I would get drunk and cry, get drunk and cry." A third was planning to keep her baby but was told she first had to pay for the hospital, the doctor, and the cost of the maternity home and counseling. She had just been laid off from her job and there was no way. Feeling utterly defeated, she signed the papers, surrendered her son, then went out and drank until she threw up.

After Fessler's book was published, she received a note from a woman about the experience of learning she had a sibling her mother had given up for adoption long ago. Her mother was in the hospital on her deathbed and cried out, "bring me my baby." Later, in a lucid moment before she passed away, she confirmed what she had gone through decades earlier. Her daughter wrote, "In that moment at the hospital, her entire life made sense to me. She was a woman who had a sense of sadness and longing her whole life. It burdens me beyond comprehension to think of her sadness and despair and of her never being able to speak of it or share it with anyone."

Chapter 46

The effect on Julie of having to give up her only child, never to see him again, to be raised by strangers, is unknown. At this point it is unknowable. Did she get over it quickly and get on with her life? Not all birth mothers were affected as profoundly as those featured in Fessler's book. Many regretted the loss of the child, but they came to grips with the fact that adoption was the best choice and went on to live happy, productive lives and have other children that they kept and raised.

Julie was just 18 when I was born. She returned to Washington University and graduated on time with her class three years later. But that does not mean she was unaffected. Brenda Davis, Julie's roommate during her years in Denver, said there was always a sadness about her. Was giving me up the cause? Did she suffer over it during the rest of her college years? And all the years that followed? Late at night, in the dorm, while others slept, did she lie awake and wonder what happened to me? Who adopted me? Where we lived? Whether the couple who became my parents were good to me? After graduation, when her friends had children and she went to their baby showers, did she think about me? When she held their babies, did her mind take her back to the summer of 1957? To the eight days when I was hers before she signed the papers? Did she hold me during those eight days? Did she feed me? When she reached her forties and knew I was in my twenties, did she wonder what had become of me? Did she ever think about trying to find me?

In Julie's case the feelings of loss may have been compounded by later events. She had become pregnant before her 18th birthday, when she was just starting college, and had a baby she couldn't keep the following summer. She returned to school, pretended nothing had happened, and hid the truth from her friends. A decade later, when she was married and wanted to start a family, she was unable to get pregnant. She had a baby when it was the last thing she wanted and couldn't have one when it was what she wanted most. What toll did it all take?

And did that toll lead to Julie's downward spiral into alcoholism? Studies show that grief is often the triggering condition that leads to a lifetime of substance abuse. The lure of turning to a mind-altering substance as a means of escape, be it drugs or alcohol, can be seductive. Alcohol is a depressant itself and aggravates the underlying grief, which may increase the desire to drink even more. Over time the body's tolerance for alcohol increases and it takes more to achieve the same effect. Excessive drinking causes many serious health problems and frequently leads to early death. Julie died of liver failure when she was only 47. She was just six months older than I was when I learned she was my mother.

Chapter 47

Carrie and I have gone on a live music cruise called Cayamo nearly every year since we met. We go for the music, not for the cruise, and the music on Cayamo is wonderful. Our first cruise was our honeymoon in 2011. In January 2013 Margie flew from Fort Lauderdale to Jackson to stay with Daddy so we could fly from Jackson to Fort Lauderdale to go on Cayamo.

The cruise that year was one of the best ever, with a lineup of artists that included Lyle Lovett, Jason Isbell, and Hayes Carll. Another of my favorites was Mary Gauthier, a great singer-songwriter and native of Louisiana. Like me, Mary was born in New Orleans and given up for adoption there. Unlike me, being surrendered by her birth mother troubled her. She wrote and recorded an entire album about it called *The Foundling*. I spoke to Mary briefly on the cruise about our similar origins. After I got home, I wrote her a long email about the story of my adoption and about learning that Julie was my mother. I had told the story many times but had never written it. At the end I said I hoped she might write a song about it.

Having taken the time to write the story, I forwarded it to a number of friends, including a lawyer with an unusual nickname, Doc Schneider of Atlanta. Doc is an outstanding lawyer who also happens to be a very talented songwriter. Mary Gauthier didn't write the song I'd hoped for, but Doc started writing one soon after I sent him the story.

Daddy died five months after we got home from the cruise and I sent his obituary to Doc along with an account of the last two years of Daddy's life with Carrie and me, when she fed him and loved him and spoiled him.

Doc read the obituary and about Daddy's time with us and sent me this message:

```
In your Dickensian tale, your wonderful
tribute to your daddy takes the cake—and
well it should. The man had a heart as
big as the Milky Way. I love your story
and how you found Carrie and how you
and Carrie took care of your daddy. And
how he lasted as long as he did on this
earth, like a river of love. I have not
forgotten your story or your song and
your daddy's goodbye is the light I need
to finish it right.
```

Several months later Doc finished his song. He called it "Baby Boy Francis" and had it professionally recorded. I cried the first time I heard it. In Doc's song Julie never recovers from the loss of her only child.

When Baby Boy Francis was born in this world,
Julie had to give him way.
And the weight of that sorrow just weighed on that girl,
giving Baby Boy Francis away.
Meanwhile the girl with the weight of the world
Fell through a hole in a glass.
She never got over the giving away,
She never knew what came to pass.

The primary theme of the song, however, is not Julie's pain. More than that it is a tribute to Mama and Daddy for loving me as if I were their own flesh and blood. And perhaps most of all, it is a song of gratitude to Julie for the great gift she gave me by giving me away.

Margaret and Paul loved that baby so much,
more than found fortune or fame.
They loved every bit of the way that he was,
and all that they changed was his name.
All that he knew was the grace of this world
that had carried him on his way.
And he wrapped his arms round the heart of his family
that came from the giving away.
Julie, you did not forsake that boy,
though you never saw it that way.
When you surrendered your Baby Boy Francis,
you gave him the whole world that day.

I have thought a great deal about how giving up her only child affected Julie, but I have also thought about how keeping me would have affected her. When Julie died in April 1986, I was almost 29, married with a child, practicing law in Jackson. Even if Julie had kept and raised me, I would not have been living with her then. But what happened in 1986 was just the final chapter of Julie's life. The seeds of her destruction had been sown long before then. During the years when she lost control of her drinking, I was a young child. Had she kept me, I would have needed her constantly, as all young children need their mothers. And being needed may have been the one thing Julie needed, the one thing she was missing. Sid, who did everything he could to help Julie, repeatedly admitting her to rehab facilities only to see her relapse time and again, told me I was probably better off with the parents who raised me. I agreed with him, but I wonder if having a child to raise would have altered the trajectory of Julie's life. Would it have chased away her demons? Was giving up her only child the worst of her demons? The effect on Julie of giving me up is impossible to know because she is not here to ask. The effect on her of keeping me is impossible to know because she did not do it.

Chapter 48

Just as I was about to finish writing this book, I learned an amazing family story I'd never heard before. When I found out the details, I knew I had to add a chapter about it. In truth, it's worthy of an entire book. The fascinating story involves another birth mother who couldn't keep her son, another family secret, a woman of questionable virtue, the fall from grace of a man of the cloth, and his redemption in the second life he made for himself far from his home. The story, about the life and times of Harry Brooks, serves as yet another illustration of the unforeseeable ripple effects a person's actions have on all the generations that follow.

I was in my office making revisions to the manuscript one day in April 2019 when my phone rang. I didn't recognize the number, suspected a telemarketer, and let the call go to voicemail. But the message the caller left, like the one Daddy received from the New Orleans lawyer nearly 15 years earlier, was intriguing. That message was about my adoption, and this message was about another one.

The caller identified himself as Lee Cheney. He said he was from Fresno, California, and was calling because he had learned that he was my first cousin. With the benefit of DNA evidence and an extensive investigation, he had discovered that Edwin Brooks, Mama's only brother, was his biological father. I called him back immediately. We had a long talk and exchanged many emails and documents in the days that followed.

Lee is only a year older than I am and, like me, was given up for adoption immediately after he was born. But there are differences. He was adopted out of our family rather than into it and his biological parents were older than most who give up a child and much older than Julie. Edwin was born in 1912 and was 43 when Lee was born. Lee's mother was 36. She grew up in Tupelo, but she and Edwin were both living in Memphis when they were seeing each other. She had a cousin in San Francisco and went there soon after learning she was pregnant. Lee had found nothing in his search indicating that Edwin ever knew he existed. Lee was born in San Francisco and has spent his life in California. He graduated from Fresno High School and started college at Fresno State in 1974, the same year Edwin died.

Lee is related by blood to my family, but I told him that he is not related by blood to me. He already knew that; he had seen a family tree stating that Margie and I were adopted. He told me he'd met several members of our family, including his older half siblings Betti and Bentley and our first cousin Andy Anderson, who helped Marjory transport Grandma across West Texas in her casket in 1977. Andy, the son of Mama's oldest sister Elizabeth, was the lead singer in a rock and roll band in the '50s that was called the Rolling Stones on this side of the Atlantic before a different band adopted the same name on the other side. Lee also revealed that he and his wife Linda and their daughter Laura had spent a great deal of time searching historical records to learn as much as they could about our family. He had just discovered that he was a member of our family, and I had been a part of it for more than 60 years, but he knew many things I didn't know.

For example, I knew very little about the early life of our grandfather Henry Felgar Brooks, who died long before Lee and I were born, and I knew nothing at all about Dr. Brooks's family background. I knew he was born in December 1875 in Kentucky, that he was 10 years older than Grandma, and that he went by Harry. I was also aware that he had a daughter from a previous marriage, and that he never got around to telling Grandma about her. Mama had told me the story of how his secret was revealed when his long-lost daughter appeared at the parsonage in Tupelo. Mama did not tell me how Grandma reacted. By then she and Harry had been married more than a quarter of a century. Lee knew a great deal about Harry and his background that I didn't know, but he had also discovered that most of what I thought I knew was wrong.

Lee had learned that our first Brooks ancestor to come to America arrived in the last decade of the 1700s. John and Mary Brooks and their five young sons sailed from England with plans to settle in the new country, but the parents didn't make it. Both died of an epidemic that broke out aboard ship and were buried at sea. Five men on the voyage discussed the predicament and each of them agreed to take one of John and Mary's sons. When the ship landed, the men and boys scattered to five different states. The brothers never saw each other again.

Joseph, the youngest of the five, was only a few years old when he lost his parents and was permanently separated from his four brothers, but he overcame his traumatic beginning and became a prosperous farmer and community leader in Fayette County, Pennsylvania. He and his wife Dorothy raised 13 children, one of whom they named Henry. Lee and I are Henry's great-great-grandsons. Henry and his wife Susan had a son, Milton, who married Eliza Felder. Our grandfather, who was named Henry for his grandfather, was the first of Milton and Eliza's three sons. Harry's parents, like mine nearly a century later, chose his mother's maiden name for his middle name and christened him Henry Felgar Brooks. Milton died when Harry was nine, Eliza when he was 16, and he and his brothers were raised to adulthood in Fayette County by his maternal grandparents.

I knew about Harry's long-lost daughter who found him in Tupelo, but Lee had learned that she was not the only one. Harry married Rose Cochran when he was 24 and they actually had five children, though three of them died when they were children and a fourth did not reach her 40th birthday. Triss, the one who knocked on the parsonage door in the late 1930s, was the only one still living at the time. Harry had five children with each of his wives. The 10 were born over a span of 35 years, from 1886 to 1921. Harry's first grandchild, my oldest first cousin, was born in 1920. My youngest first cousin, Sid's daughter Julia, was born 74 years later. I was born exactly halfway between them.

Lee had also learned that I was wrong about where Harry was born. I had seen records, including Mama's birth certificate, showing that he was born in Kentucky, but he was actually born in western Pennsylvania. I was also wrong about Harry's age and date of birth and not by just a year or two. He was not born on December 29, 1875, as both his gravestone in the cemetery in Carlton, Texas, and a number of records indicate, but in truth was born nearly 14 years earlier. He came into the world on New Year's Day 1862, less than a year after the Civil War began and 18 months before the pivotal battle of Gettysburg not far to the east of his birthplace. Harry was about to turn 81 when he died, not 67 as his gravestone reflects. Records indicate that he was 45 when Mama and Marjory became his last two children in March 1921, but he was actually 59. Like me, the twins were fortunate to be born at all. A man approaching 60 who has already fathered eight children rarely has two more.

Grandma refused on grounds of principle and privacy to disclose her age, instead revealing only that she was as old as her tongue but older than her teeth. Harry took a more radical approach, deciding at some point not to conceal his age but to lie about it. Now, more than 75 years after his death, there is no way to know exactly when he made the decision. Nor is he here to explain why. One possibility is that he wanted churches looking to hire a preacher to think he was younger than he was, but two other reasons seem more likely. He may have wanted to be more appealing not to churches as a prospective preacher but to the woman he was courting as a prospective husband. Ethel was 24 when they married in early 1910. Harry would have been 34 if he was born at the end of 1875, the revised date of birth he gave himself and carried to his grave, but he was actually 48, exactly twice Ethel's age. Had she known the truth, she might have rejected his proposal. Even if she had accepted it, her parents might have withheld their consent. Ethel was born in Mississippi only a month before Harry married Rose Cochran in Pennsylvania, and his oldest child, Triss, was born only 10 months later. He and his first wife were a full generation older than his second wife.

The second possible motive—and what makes the story worthy

of a separate book—is that Harry lied about the date and place of his birth to make it more difficult for anyone to investigate his troubled past and find out the truth. Lee told me the fascinating story of our grandfather, about which I knew absolutely nothing, and sent me documents and newspaper reports confirming the details.

Harry had received a fine education from his grandfather and became a capable schoolteacher, principal, and administrator. He was often referred to in the press as Professor Brooks. He was also active in the church and was called into the ministry at an early age in the Indian Creek congregation. The *Biographical and Historical Society of Westmoreland County* published in 1890 described Harry as "an intelligent, industrious, energetic young man of noble ambition and high aspirations." His fellow citizens confirmed that they held him in high regard by electing him shortly after the turn of the century to serve as the superintendent of schools for McKeesport and Uniontown, southeast of Pittsburgh.

But at some point Harry lost his way, perhaps because of the tragic loss of three young children or the struggle to support a grieving wife from a prominent family on a modest salary. Or perhaps, as a contemporaneous history suggests, the cause of his downfall was living beyond his means in an effort to achieve social standing. The *History of the Church of the Brethren of the Western District of Pennsylvania*, published in 1916, states without elaboration that Harry "gave promise of great usefulness to the church, but moving in high society caused his ruin."

But whatever his motive, Harry's misconduct was clear. He gave in to temptation while working as the school superintendent and embezzled $2,000, pocketing tuition payments rather than turning them over to the school district. The amount may seem insignificant today, but $2,000 then would be worth nearly thirty times as much now.

And the embezzlement was not the last of Harry's misdeeds. After taking the money, he left town with an acquaintance from Pittsburgh, Bess Montgomery, who was described by a newspaperman as "a woman of doubtful repute." Harry's second misdeed led to his capture and punishment for his first. The sheriff of Fayette County tracked Bess down, "sweated" her according to the same reporter, and she told all. She revealed both that Harry was on his way to Liverpool on a Cunard liner and that he was traveling under an assumed name, H. B. Telfer. The local newspaper published an article detailing Harry's wrongdoing and whereabouts while he was still in route. Because he was in the middle of the Atlantic, he did not get word of the article and was unaware of what awaited him at the end of his journey. He grew a full beard, presumably as a disguise to help him make a clean getaway, but his efforts were for naught. Officers from Scotland Yard were waiting when the ship docked at Queenstown on the south shore of Ireland before reaching its ultimate destination. They arrested Harry and put him in jail.

The sheriff and an investigator then followed Harry across the Atlantic to bring him back to Pennsylvania to stand trial. The sheriff had a personal stake in the matter; he had loaned Harry nearly $500, which remained unpaid. A court in London issued an extradition order and the officers and their prisoner then re-crossed the ocean, docking in New York City at midnight on Wednesday, August 30, 1905. A reporter who accompanied them on the train from New York to Uniontown wrote that the strain on Professor Brooks was evident and that "he gazed out the window of the train car in a moody silence." When they arrived, Harry expected one of his brothers to be there to post bond to secure his release, but he was disappointed when neither brother appeared. He remained in jail and was soon tried and convicted.

At his sentencing hearing in January 1906 Harry expressed his deep regret. "Your Honor, when I say that I'm sorry the word does not express my feeling. The mental anguish which I felt at times was more than I could bear. My ambitions were along another line, and I'm sorry beyond expression. It was never my intention to embezzle any money and I had hoped to meet all my obligations some time. I shall consider my obligations just as binding, whatever may be my lot." The newspaper article reporting on the matter was headlined "BROOKS WAS SORRY." Maybe he was, but an apology wasn't good enough. The trial judge fined Harry $400 and sentenced him to the state prison for two years and 10 months. He reported to the penitentiary on March 20, 1906.

When Harry was released after serving his term, he wanted to turn over a new leaf and prove himself worthy of a second chance, but forgiveness and redemption were not to be found in his home state. Not surprisingly, Rose had divorced him, and his own family had disowned him. He was not even mentioned in his brothers' obituaries when they died years later. He concluded that his only choice was to leave the only home he'd ever known and start over somewhere new. He could not have known that his new life, like his old one, would include a wife and five children. Nor could he have known that he would be able to spend the rest of his life preaching the Gospel, ministering to congregants who knew nothing of his past.

Harry left Pennsylvania and headed southwest to Texas, where he soon met Ethel Land. Their wedding took place only a year after he was released from prison. But Harry almost certainly kept his recent troubles a secret from his new bride. Mama knew that he didn't tell Grandma about either his first wife or his daughter, so surely he didn't tell her that he'd served nearly three years behind bars for embezzlement or that he'd fled the scene of the crime with another woman and tried to escape to Europe. The better course may have been to disclose the whole truth and ask Ethel for sympathy and understanding, but a complete confession would have posed grave risks. She might not have been sympathetic and she might not have kept the story to herself. Confiding in her could have ended not only their relationship but also his calling as a preacher. Some relatives heard rumors over the years about past troubles, perhaps originating with Triss, but that was all. Grandma and all five of their children almost certainly went to their graves without knowing the details of the story Lee uncovered. Nor did others know. The photo of Harry giving the prayer before FDR's speech in Tupelo in 1934 bears a handwritten note stating that Roosevelt addressed "acres of people." No one in the huge crowd knew of Harry's troubled past. No one but Harry. Fortunately for him, there was no internet a century ago.

So Harry almost certainly lived the second half of his life in fear
that the dark secrets from the first half would come to light. He
must have been terrified when Triss showed up unannounced at
the parsonage. She was 18 when Harry fled to Europe, 19 when
he was sentenced to prison, and 22 when he was released and fled
to Texas. She must have known the whole story. But his secret
remained hidden and he continued to serve as a revered minister
of the Word of God for the rest of his life. Perhaps he confessed it
all to Grandma after Triss showed up, but there's no way to know.
All we know is that she stayed by his side.

And with her by his side, Harry by all accounts lived an upstand-
ing life from the time of his arrival in Texas until his death. As their
family grew during the first 10 years of their marriage, he served
as the pastor of churches in desolate West Texas. For his last two
decades, after Grandma prevailed on him to bring her back to the
state where she was born and raised, he was the senior minister
of Methodist churches in Jackson and a series of towns in north
Mississippi. When President Roosevelt came to town in 1934, it
was Harry Brooks rather than one of Tupelo's many other preachers
who was chosen to give the invocation. The following year, 30 years
after Scotland Yard arrested him on the dock in Queenstown, Harry
gave FDR advice about who should be eligible for the WPA. The
year after that, three decades after beginning his prison sentence, he
wrote beautifully of Tupelo's recovery from the devastating tornado.
Late in life he was chosen to serve as a senior official of the North
Mississippi Methodist Conference, which provided significant
support to the home for unwed mothers in New Orleans where
two of his grandchildren were born long after he died.

In addition to his work as a minister, Harry was selected one
year to serve as a delegate to the Congress of the American Prison
Association. He must have had to bite his tongue as he sat through
meetings in which other delegates who had never set foot in a prison
held forth on the state of America's penal system and what should
be done to improve it. Harry had turned his life around and found
redemption by then, but he almost certainly did not reveal to the
other delegates why he knew more about prison life than they did.

The life of brilliant Texas songwriter Blaze Foley was cut short when he was shot to death in Austin at the age of 39 by the son of a friend. One of his most beautiful songs, "Clay Pigeons," was recorded years after his death by John Prine, the magnificent song-writer and American treasure. When Prine covers a song, you know it's a good one. In the fourth verse the narrator speaks of longing to stay but needing to start over again, perhaps down in Texas or someplace he'd never been.

Harry Brooks died before Blaze was born and more than three decades before he wrote "Clay Pigeons." The song is not about Harry, but it could be. Harry couldn't stay in Pennsylvania, started over in Texas, and then went to Mississippi, somewhere that he'd never been.

And the improbable second half of Harry's life was the result of a series of improbable events in the first. The sheriff was able to identify and find Bess Montgomery only because he discovered that Harry had bought her a dress. If Harry had not bought the dress, the sheriff would not have found her and she would not have revealed Harry's escape plans. And because nobody would have known where to look for him, Harry almost certainly would have walked off the ship with the rest of the passengers when it reached Liverpool. The second life he made for himself would have been in the country his ancestors had left behind more than a century earlier, not in Texas and not in Mississippi.

The future would have unfolded differently in other ways as well. In the summer of 1905, when middle-aged Harry Brooks was crossing the Atlantic to escape from the law, Ethel Land was a teenager living on a farm with her parents southwest of Fort Worth. Had he not bought the dress, Harry would not have gotten caught, would not have served time, would not have gone to Texas, and would not have married Ethel. And, with but two exceptions, their children, grandchildren, and great-grandchildren never would have come into the world. Margie and I still would have been born in New Orleans, but we would not have been adopted by Paul and Margaret Eason because there would have been no Margaret Eason. Our lives would be different, our spouses would almost certainly be different, and our children and grandchildren would not be the ones that we have. And but for the purchase of a dress, my new cousin Lee Cheney and the new family he found would not exist.

Chapter 49

Carrie and I love hosting house concerts, which makes Camp Carrie our favorite local live music venue. Our second favorite is Duling Hall, which was the auditorium in what used to be an elementary school in an old neighborhood in Jackson. In January 2016 Carrie and I went there for a concert by one of our favorite artists, Robert Earl Keen, but we wound up not getting to hear him sing a single song.

As we stood listening to the opening act, I noticed something wrong with my left arm. There was no pain and it wasn't numb, but it felt like a dead weight attached to my shoulder, like it needed a place to rest. I walked over and rested it on the bar. Between acts Carrie demanded that I describe my symptoms to a friend who was with us, Ashley Seawright, an accomplished nurse practitioner. Ashley said it sounded like a stroke or a heart attack. She instructed us to leave immediately and go straight to the emergency room at the University of Mississippi Medical Center, the teaching hospital where she works. It was the same hospital where I'd refused to get out of the ambulance when I wrecked my Beetle three decades earlier. She said she would call ahead and they would be waiting. I protested—Robert Earl was about to play—but I was no match for Ashley and Carrie, the expert and wife. As we walked to the car, I heard the crowd as Robert Earl took the stage.

Two nurses greeted us at the entrance to the ER, directed me to a bed, and began to examine me. It seemed like much ado about very little. I was more annoyed about missing the concert than worried about my health. My speech and vision were fine and, unlike after my wreck in 1986, I answered all their questions correctly. It was just my arm.

Soon they got a wheelchair and rolled me out for a CAT scan, then brought me back to wait for the results. Before long a young doctor appeared with the verdict. He was from Egypt; his name was Kareem. He declared that I'd had a stroke. I told him I felt fine and asked if he was sure. He said he was positive, that it happened several hours earlier. I said we were leaving on vacation the next day, flying to Miami for our annual music cruise. It was paid for and non-refundable and I felt okay. Could we still go? Kareem smiled and said, "afraid not." I would be staying with them for a few days. I was 58 years old, the same age when my grandmother Betty had a stroke.

I was soon moved to a regular room, where I was awakened during the night and wheeled out for another test, this time an MRI. It was my first of four. That was four too many as far as I was concerned. Being stuck in the MRI tube with the loud clanging made me feel claustrophobic. In the morning the symptoms of the stroke were worse. My left hand was uncoordinated and the left side of my face felt strange. I poked myself in the eye washing my hair in the shower and bit the inside of my lip eating breakfast.

While Carrie was at home changing clothes and getting some things for me, the head of the neurology department came in to tell me about the MRI results. He had a machine to show me the slides and he spoke with a thick German accent. A young man and woman were with him. I assumed they were med students or residents.

He began by saying I'd actually had four strokes. He showed me four slides of my brain with tiny spots, each of which he said was a stroke, and he identified the one that was causing my symptoms. I asked if they happened simultaneously and he said there was no way to know. Before showing me the next slide, he paused and said, "But of greater concern is this."

Then he showed me the fifth slide, which revealed some sort of abnormality that was many times the size of the four tiny strokes. It appeared to cover nearly a fourth of my brain. When I asked what it was, he was matter of fact. "In all likelihood it is either an infection or cancer. Cancer is more common and you have no sign of an infection." I'm sure he's a brilliant man, but I found his bedside manner lacking. I let the news sink in and then asked what was next. He said they would perform a number of tests to reach a definitive diagnosis. His assistants would explain the details. With that he was gone.

I am a stoic for the most part, or at least I try to act like one, and I listened calmly as they described all the tests. Carrie returned soon after they left and I shared the news with her. She did not accept it as calmly as I did. So that I wouldn't see, she went down to the parking lot, sat in the car by herself, and cried.

But it turned out the doctor was wrong. They did all the tests, including two more MRIs, another CAT scan, a spinal tap, and other unpleasant procedures the details of which I've blocked from my memory, and they found no sign of cancer. They decided a tumor was unlikely, though they still couldn't rule it out, and there was still no sign of infection. When I was discharged three days later, my hand and face were improving, but I still had the large, mysterious spot on my brain. They had no idea what it was and scheduled me for yet another MRI in several weeks to check it again. If the spot was smaller, that would be good news, if it was the same they would schedule another MRI, and if it was larger they would drill a hole in my skull and do a biopsy.

Several days after I returned for my fourth MRI, Carrie and I went to the hospital's department of neurological oncology to get the results. I was still a stoic; she was still nervous. We were greeted by a young doctor we hadn't seen before. He had hair like Kramer on *Seinfeld* and his lab coat was covered with stains. He reported that the MRI showed improvement. Carrie squeezed my leg and asked what that meant. The spot, he said, had disappeared. I said that sounded like good news and asked him what the spot had been. He said he didn't know and now there was no way to find out. After all, he repeated, it was gone. I was released from the hospital's care and my future appointments were canceled. And the spot that was there on one MRI and gone the next remains a mystery to this day.

My hand and face were soon back to normal and I was hiking in the mountains of Colorado by Labor Day. Physically I was back to my pre-stroke condition, but the experience had changed my outlook on life. Nothing concentrates the mind like being told you probably have a brain tumor. During the weeks when my future was still in doubt, I had time to think about how much time I had left on Earth and what I wanted to do with it. And I decided that, whatever my future held, I wanted to spend less of it practicing law and selling my time by the tenth of an hour and more of it doing things I enjoy. To make that possible, I worked out an arrangement with my law firm to work less and make less. It was liberating.

Chapter 50

One of the things I've done with my additional free time is learn about Julie from her friends and family to help me write this story. In early 2018 I reached out to a number of people who'd known Julie well. All were generous with their time and some with more than that. I spoke to Lewis Bettman, corresponded with him often, and Carrie and I had lunch with him in St. Louis. I should have asked him for the dollar he was supposed to give me from Julie's estate, but I forgot. Lewis suggested I track down Brenda Davis and talk to her. I found her with a quick search of the internet, wrote her a letter telling her that I was Julie's son, and then spoke to her at length. I also called Sid Smith and asked if Carrie and I could come to Tulsa for a visit. He agreed immediately and we scheduled a trip in April. I was initially unsuccessful in finding Lee Farnham, but Sid remembered that he had gone to Middlebury College and I found his name, including middle initial, on a list of donors to the school. I then located a Lee Farnham in New Jersey with the same middle initial. I emailed him, said I was Julie's son, and asked if he was the Lee Farnham who'd been married to her. My phone rang immediately, and we had a long talk and later corresponded often. I also spoke on the phone to Sandy Buell and then met her, her son Pearson, and his wife Lisa in the suburb of St. Louis where they live.

Writing about the mother I didn't know has been a challenge. There is still a great deal about Julie I don't know, but I learned many things about her from those who did. I learned about the places she lived and trips she took and about her beauty, intelligence, kindness, and generosity. I also learned about her alcoholism and how it led to her early death. And I found out that, with few exceptions, she concealed the fact that she had a baby when she was 18 even from those to whom she was very close.

Brenda lived with Julie in Denver when they were in their early twenties, just a few years after I was born. The roommates must have confided in each other about many things, but Julie never breathed a word about the baby she had in New Orleans in 1957. As a result, Brenda did not learn that Julie had a son until she received my letter more than 60 years after Julie gave birth to me. The revelation made Brenda think back to their years in Denver, to a time when Julie should have had it all and yet always seemed to have a sadness about her. Was it shame because she had a baby out of wedlock? Was it regret because she gave me away? Was it worry because she didn't know what happened to me?

Brenda told me there would have been no debate about what to do, not in the late 1950s for an 18-year-old girl from a prominent family. When Ann Lowrey got pregnant with Ada Brooks nearly 50 years later, she had options. She could have given her baby up for adoption as Julie did, or she could have had an abortion as Bio and his parents wanted. She also had the option she chose, the option to have and keep her baby. Julie didn't have all the options Ann Lowrey had.

Pregnancy termination rates have declined in recent years, but 15 percent of all pregnancies in America still end in abortion. Studies estimate that nearly one in four American women will have an abortion at some point in their lives. Whatever a person's views may be on the legality of abortion—that they should be illegal from the moment of conception, legal until the moment before birth, or something in between—the 60 million pregnancies that have ended in abortion since *Roe v. Wade* are nothing to celebrate. Not surprisingly, abortions far outnumber adoptions. The ratio of terminated pregnancies to infant adoptions in the country is now 40–to–one.

But abortion was not readily available when Julie got pregnant with me. In the 1950s abortion was illegal in nearly every state, including Oklahoma, Missouri, and Louisiana, the states where Julie grew up, went to college, and was sent to have her baby. It's no coincidence that Methodist Home Hospital in New Orleans ceased to be a home for unwed mothers only months after the Supreme Court decided *Roe v. Wade* in January 1973. If the case had been decided two decades earlier, it would have been a simple matter for Julie to find an abortion clinic, undergo the procedure, and return to class. Nobody would have had to know, not her parents and not even the father. And although some women who have abortions suffer lasting emotional harm, perhaps having an abortion would have been less traumatic for Julie than carrying me to term, giving birth to me, and then giving me away to be raised by a couple she never met. But an abortion would have affected more than just Julie and would have meant more than just the end of me. My three children and four grandchildren would not exist and all the lives they have touched would be different. Paul the Groom would have a different wife and children and there would be no St. Augustine School and no Grand Prize.

Not only was abortion illegal, but Julie almost certainly could not have kept me either. Of the million and a half unwed girls and young women who were sent to maternity homes in the generation between the end of World War II and 1973, more than 80 percent of them gave their babies up for adoption. Today there is Feminists for Life, which is dedicated to providing women with resources and support so they don't feel compelled to choose abortion. Half a century ago there was no similar organization devoted to helping unwed mothers so they didn't feel compelled to choose adoption. And the assumption shared by those in a position to help—parents, friends, and the staff at maternity homes—was that adoption was the obvious choice, that the baby would be better off with a mature married couple than with a young single mother. That was undoubtedly true in many cases, but not in every case.

The mothers interviewed by Ann Fessler for *The Girls Who Went Away* reported almost uniformly that they felt they had no choice in the matter. Most of the women told Fessler they were never asked to make a decision. One complained bitterly that she had never harmed a child before or since and there was no reason to take her baby away from her, but that didn't matter. It was all about what people would think. Another woman told Fessler, "I was powerless because I was 17 and unmarried. Society and my church and my parents felt that was the right decision for me. I had no voice."

Like the woman who told Fessler she had no voice, Julie was 17 and unmarried when she got pregnant. She was also the granddaughter of the chairman of the board of Ozark Mahoning Company and the stepdaughter of the president of Sinclair Oil Company. For her to keep and raise a child born out of wedlock would have been unthinkable. The only option was for Julie to drop out of school, leave St. Louis, and go to a maternity home. So that's what she did. There were places girls were sent. Methodist Home Hospital—the "Institution of Mercy That They Might Have Life"—was one of them. Brenda told me the names of some of the others. The girls were gone for months and then returned. Friends suspected why, but as a rule they didn't ask and the girls didn't tell.

Thinking about Ann Lowrey's and Julie's experiences and reading the stories in Ann Fessler's book made me think of a sad but wonderful song by John Prine. The song, "Unwed Fathers," vividly describes the differences in how society viewed unwed mothers and unwed fathers and the consequences they faced. In the song a scared teenage girl leaves home on a Greyhound bus for a cold and gray town, where she has her baby in a gray stone building surrounded by strangers. The unwed father, who can't be bothered, doesn't go with her and does nothing for her. He runs from the consequences of his actions like water in a mountain stream.

I told Brenda about Ann Lowrey and Ada Brooks and the similarities between their story and the story of Julie and me. Brenda said it's much better now. Not only did girls in the '50s have no say about what happened, but there was still a stigma associated with being born out of wedlock, with being a bastard, as if the child was somehow to blame. I was reminded of the picnic-table meeting with Bio and his parents, of his father saying that Ann Lowrey shouldn't want to bring a bastard into the world. He knew

I was adopted. His wife was too. I'm a bastard. She probably is too. I wonder if that even occurred to him.

Julie likewise never told Lewis Bettman about the baby she had in New Orleans. He said he suspected Julie was pregnant. Why else would she leave school after the first semester of her freshman year and not return until the fall? But it was not a gentleman's place to ask and, through nearly three decades of friendship that lasted the rest of her life, she never told him. Lewis did not find out that Julie had a son until he located her will, the will in which she named him the executor of her estate. She entrusted him with her assets but not with her secret.

Julie didn't even tell her own brother, her only biological sibling. Like Lewis, Sid learned about me for the first time when he read Julie's will. Sid told Carrie and me that he had moved to Florida with Julie and Betty for several months when he was young. He didn't know why, though it must have been because Julie was pregnant, and he didn't remember exactly where. He just knew it was in Florida on the beach and he liked it. Carrie asked Sid what he recalled about their time at the beach. He remembered one day when a crowd gathered to watch a struggle offshore between a whale and a giant squid, but he did not remember that Julie gained weight or had other symptoms of pregnancy. Nor would he. He was seven years old. He did not turn eight until nine days before I was born. He was exactly the same age I was when I went on my first trip to the West with Mama, Daddy, and Margie in the summer of 1965. A boy that age is much more likely to remember a whale and a squid than whether his sister put on weight or had morning sickness.

Of Julie's friends and family members I spoke to in order to write this book, Lee Farnham was one of only two who learned about me during Julie's lifetime, but he knew very little. People say things when drinking they wouldn't when sober, often things they later regret. One evening, after several gin and tonics, Julie and Lee were swapping stories from their pasts. Lee spoke about two old girlfriends and Julie responded by telling him that she got pregnant while at Washington University. She said she dropped out of school for nine months, went to New Orleans, and had a baby boy. That's all she said and neither of them ever brought up the subject again.

It's interesting that Julie never spoke to her brother about having a baby and never told Brenda, her friend and roommate, or Lewis, to whom she was close from their college days until her death. And yet she told her husband, seemingly the last person a woman would want to know. Perhaps it was a burden she needed to lay down, to share, something too important to keep from the man she loved. Or perhaps she was upset by hearing of Lee's old girlfriends and responded by saying she not only had a boyfriend but he got her pregnant. She did not tell Lee who the boyfriend was.

The one other person Julie shared her secret with was Sandy Buell. Julie thought of Sandy as much more than a stepsister. From the time their parents married when Julie was eight and Sandy 10, the two shared a room until Sandy left for Massachusetts to attend Smith College. The two remained close the rest of Julie's life, visiting each other at every chance and going on wonderful trips together. There was no one Julie loved more. When Julie asked a lawyer in Aspen to prepare her will in 1978, she chose to leave her jewelry to Sandy and the rest of her estate to Sandy's three sons if she was no longer married.

And when Julie got pregnant in the fall of 1956, it was Sandy to whom she turned for comfort and support. She swore Sandy to secrecy and Sandy kept her promise. She never told a soul. Nor did she bring up the subject of Julie's baby when the two of them were alone together. But there were times, as the years went by, when Julie did. Sometimes, late at night, when everyone else was asleep and it was just the two sisters, Julie would talk about her baby, the baby she had to give away, the son she knew by then would be her only child. Sandy was an adoptee herself—she and one of her older brothers had been adopted by Herb and Miriam Smith—and she would cite her own experience to reassure Julie. I can imagine one of their conversations.

"I wonder where he is. He would be 16 by now. Driving. My son would be driving. You think he has a good family, parents who love him?"

"You know he does. Good parents adopt children. Good parents adopted me."

"I'm sure you're right, but I wonder. I could have given him so much. I wonder what his name is. I don't even know his name."

"You were 18. You didn't have a husband. You didn't have a choice."

"I know, but I still wonder. I can't help but wonder."

Then Sandy would take Julie's hands, look at her, and say, "I'm sure he's alright. I'm sure of it."

But Sandy would be thinking she would wonder too, that she would wonder every single day.

More than 60 years after Julie gave me away, Sandy told Carrie and me that Julie would have been a wonderful mother. But Sandy also said that nobody would have taken her baby away from her if she had been the one who had gotten pregnant. In those days, however, could she really have kept her baby? Could she have done what other girls like her weren't allowed to do? She could have tried, though it seems doubtful she would have succeeded. But even if she was wrong about being able to keep a baby, she was right to reassure Julie about me. I had good parents; I was alright. As for whether Julie would have been a wonderful mother, it's impossible to know because she never got the chance to try.

Chapter 51

While trying to find out more about where I was born, I came across a wonderful Facebook page that was established for the birth mothers sent to Methodist Home Hospital and the children who were born there. It was on Facebook that I learned that the home was founded in 1886, the same year my biological great-grandparents Sidney and Minnie Davis and my adoptive grandmother Ethel Land Brooks were born and Harry Brooks married for the first time. The Facebook page is also where I read the brochure that called the home "An Institution of Mercy Supported by the Methodist Church That They Might Have Life."

The experiences shared by the birth mothers on Facebook revealed that they were sent to the home not just to have their babies and not just to give them up for adoption but also to hide their pregnancies and their shame from the world. The same brochure described an unwed girl's unwanted pregnancy as "the darkest hour that ever comes to any family." Unlike the joy Ann Lowrey experienced when Ada Brooks was born, there was nothing joyous for an unwed mother about bringing a baby into the world half a century earlier. One mother from the home wrote of being given the twilight drug and waking up in a room with a stranger in the bed next to hers. She learned her baby was a girl when a nurse brought her to be fed. She later had to walk down the hall to a pay phone, call her parents, and tell them. There was no joy or celebration, just overwhelming sadness and shame. Adding to the shame, when girls packed up their things and left their babies behind at the home, they were given written instructions to "go forth and sin no more."

Girls, and most of them were too young to be considered women, were sent to the home before they started to show, when they were only three or four months pregnant. As an added precaution to help keep it all a secret, they were given aliases to be used during their time there. Many women on the Facebook page remembered the names they were told to use. To explain her whereabouts, one birth mother reported that she and her family claimed she had left home to attend Draughon's Business College. Another revealed that she used the same cover story.

The act of turning over babies to their adoptive parents was also handled with secrecy and discretion. Though some adoptive parents picked up their babies at the home, other babies were brought to their new parents in rooms at the Roosevelt Hotel. Some adoptive parents were even given their babies in parks. In one case a staff member arranged to meet the couple on the corner of Bourbon Street and Esplanade and gave them their new baby there. A man posted a home movie made in a room at the Capri Motel in 1963 showing a woman placing an infant in an adoptive mother's arms for the first time. The man who posted the movie was the baby, the movie maker his adoptive father.

One member of the group posted a copy of a letter from New Orleans lawyer Max Schaumburger, the same lawyer who handled my adoption. I have an almost identical letter from him on the same stationery. Two sisters wrote that they had babies in the home several years apart and gave them both up for adoption. One birth mother revealed that she had been a statewide officer in a church youth organization in Louisiana and declared that she had embarrassed the whole state. Another responded that she had been an officer in the same organization in Mississippi.

Many of the birth mothers Ann Fessler interviewed for *The Girls Who Went Away* had found their lost children decades after giving them up for adoption and many others were still searching. That was true of the mothers from Methodist Home Hospital as well. On Facebook I read the stories of many successful reunions—birth mothers finding their children, children finding their birth mothers, siblings finding each other. Many were assisted by volunteer "search angels," kind women who examine records and provide advice about DNA testing. Family members wrote of the excitement they felt as they anticipated reunions they were about to have. A woman who was born in the home two years before I was born there learned that she was the oldest of at least nine siblings and perhaps as many as 11. One mother had searched for 12 years and had just found her daughter. Some members of the group posted photos and videos of their reunions. A birth mother I spoke to said she was overwhelmed when she was found by her son 49 years after she gave birth to him. They talked on the phone for four hours and she told him she had thought about him every day of his life.

Not all reunions described on the Facebook page were happy, however, and not all efforts to reunite were welcome. Some children found by their birth mothers resented being given up for adoption and just wanted to be left alone, and some birth mothers found by their children wanted what had always been a secret to remain a secret. And not all efforts to find children and birth parents had been successful. On July 3, 2018, a birth mother posted birthday wishes to the daughter she was still trying to find exactly half a century after she was born. Her daughter and I share the same birthplace and birthday. I hope her mother finds her.

I asked the women on the Methodist Home Hospital Facebook page if they remembered any black birth mothers during their time in the home. They remembered very few, but the facility did not exclude them, at least not in its later years. One explanation for the disparity in numbers is that out-of-wedlock births in the black community were not regarded with the same degree of shame and obsession with secrecy. Black families were more likely to support their pregnant daughters and keep them at home, and most black babies who could not be raised by their young mothers were taken into the extended family rather than given up for adoption. Finances also played a role. Many black families were unable to afford even the modest cost of maternity homes. For all of these reasons white mothers surrendered babies at ten times the rate of black mothers in the two decades before *Roe v. Wade*. But there were exceptions. Some black preachers' daughters were sent to the home in New Orleans and several birth mothers recalled Marie, a sweet black girl who was in the home waiting to have her baby when her mother died. Her mother's dying wish was that poor Marie be barred from the funeral, no doubt to spare the rest of the woman's family the embarrassment of having her pregnant daughter at the service.

Birth mothers from the home reported different experiences with their babies during the days before they surrendered them and returned to their hometowns. To limit the pain of giving up her baby, one mother chose neither to look at her daughter nor hold her. She saw her and touched her for the first time when they were reunited nearly five decades later. Another said she was permitted to hold her son for only 15 minutes before he was taken away. A third birth mother reported that she was given nearly an hour, prayed the whole time, then rode with her parents the three hours back to their hometown with none of them saying a word. Still another one described the depth of her reaction when she held her baby for the first time, writing that it cracked her wide open and shattered her heart. Which is more painful for a new mother, choosing never to see and hold her baby or seeing and holding her baby just once but never again?

The women in Fessler's book reported time and again that the birth of the baby changed everything. Before the delivery the birth mother thought of the pregnancy as a problem, a mistake, the consequences of an unfortunate accident. But suddenly there was a child, *her* child. Some tried to change their minds about giving their babies up but were not permitted to do so. Others, like the mother who had the baby Tommy and Addie Louis thought would be theirs, were successful in keeping their babies. A birth mother I spoke to was in the home in New Orleans with a girl who demanded to keep her baby, succeeded, and was considered a heroine by all the other girls.

One of the best ways of dealing with grief is to confide in others who are experiencing the same loss and the same grief. The girls had each other to lean on when they were together but, after their babies were born and they returned to their hometowns, there was no one. Some girls tried to find and talk to others who'd lived with them in the maternity home on Washington Avenue, but the use of aliases made it impossible for most. They were alone. But now, at least on Facebook, they were no longer alone. I read many warm expressions of support—birth mothers caring for each other and acknowledging all they'd gone through. One wrote that she was grateful she could finally share the pain of her experience with others who truly understood. I thought that these women, all in their sixties or older, were getting grief counseling half a century after they needed it most.

I also learned that in recent years my birthplace had gone to the dogs, literally. In 1973, when the need for homes for unwed mothers plummeted after the Supreme Court decided *Roe v. Wade*, Methodist Home Hospital changed its mission and became a home for abused children. By the time I discovered the Facebook group, the youngest of the babies born when it was a maternity home were in their mid-forties. The home for abused children later moved to a new facility and the building on Washington Avenue became a rehabilitation center for special-needs dogs. It was called Dag's House, named for a rescue dog named Dag that inspired the owner to open it. More recently it was converted into an upscale dog spa called Belladoggie Resort Spa for Dogs.

Reading through all the posts and comments on the Facebook page made me realize how little I will ever know about all that happened in the summer of 1957 when I was born in the home on Washington Avenue. I don't know when Julie was sent to the home or how long she was there. She almost certainly had been in Florida with Betty and Sid, so she may not have been there as long as most of the girls. What alias was she given? Like some of the girls, did she refuse to use it? What did she do in the home during the time she was there? One birth mother told me girls would sit in the courtyard, smoke cigarettes, and talk about the names they would give their babies, their so-called crib names. Most of the girls in the home were teenagers and some chose to name their babies for members of the hottest bands on the radio. The girls knew the crib names were temporary, like Mary the male corgi's name was supposed to be, so they could have fun choosing them. Did Julie settle on Scott as my crib name while she was in the courtyard with the other girls? How did she decide on Scott? Could Scott have been my father's name? Like the story of Mama and Daddy's courtship, the answers to all these questions are lost in the mists of time.

Some of the pregnant girls worked in the nursery taking care of babies waiting to be adopted whose birth mothers had already left the home. How strange to enlist pregnant girls to take care of other girls' babies but give them only a few minutes with their own. I wonder if Julie worked in the nursery. I also wonder if the doctor and nurse were the only ones there when Julie went into labor and when I was born. Or was Betty or someone else there with her? And after I was born, did Julie hold me and feed me? What emotions did she feel when she left me behind in New Orleans? She was back in class in St. Louis by the time Mama and Daddy took me home to Tupelo.

Nor do I know how Julie wound up in a maternity home in south Louisiana, more than 600 miles from Tulsa and farther than that from St. Louis. The beach in Florida where she was staying with Betty and Sid may have been closer, but nearly all the birth mothers came from Louisiana and Mississippi, the states where the Methodist churches supported the home's mission. Julie was the exception. The social worker from the home told Mama that extra care had to be taken to keep my birth mother's identity a secret because she was from a prominent family. Maybe Julie was sent to a home in south Louisiana to ensure that no one would know who she was.

But whatever the reason, I'm thankful Julie was sent to New Orleans when she became one of the girls who went away. Had she gone elsewhere, Mama and Daddy would have adopted some other baby and I would be somebody else. I would not be Brooks Eason. I have no idea if I was first placed in Mama's arms in the home or a hotel room or somewhere else but, wherever it was, I am grateful they were her arms.

Carrie I spent the weekend before Christmas 2018 in New

Orleans. We stayed at the Roosevelt Hotel, which was decorated beautifully for the holidays, and one morning I walked to the corner of Bourbon Street and Esplanade. I thought about what I'd read on the Facebook page and imagined what it was like for adoptive parents as they waited in a hotel room or on a street corner for the baby that would soon be theirs.

After having brunch with friends on Sunday before we headed north toward home, Carrie and I stopped by the building on Washington Avenue that had not been a home for unwed mothers in 45 years. It was my first time to return to my birthplace since Mama and Daddy made the long drive from Tupelo after the social worker called with the news that there was a baby boy waiting for them there. The building was no longer a dog spa. It was vacant, with signs outside announcing that it was for rent. But it did not stay vacant for long. I learned in May 2019 on the Facebook page that it had just been converted into apartments and I saw photos of the remodeled interior, the windows between the hall and nursery covered over with Sheetrock. When we were there in December, the doors were locked and most of the blinds were drawn, but through a window I saw a Goo Goo Dolls poster on the wall. The band got its start in Buffalo in 1986, the same year Julie died of cirrhosis in Tulsa and I nearly died in a car wreck in Jackson.

After peering into the windows and circling the building, I read the plaque on the wall beside the front door. It stated that the home was organized in 1886 and the building was erected in 1951. At the bottom were the same words I had read in the home's brochure: An Institution of Mercy Supported by the Methodist Church That They Might Have Life. I pondered the fact that the First Methodist Church in Tupelo, where my grandfather Harry Brooks preached, Momie and Daddy Cliff and Mama and Daddy were lifelong members, and Margie and I grew up, supported the home as an act of mercy for girls like Julie and children like Margie and me.

Later Carrie and I walked the streets around the home and I imagined what it was like more than six decades earlier for Julie to walk these same streets as she spent her days waiting for the birth of the child she would have to give away. The neighborhood appeared to have changed little. The live oaks would have been smaller and the houses newer, but they were the same trees and the same houses because all of them were more than 60 years old. I wondered what Julie thought about when she walked the streets of the neighborhood in the heat that summer, sometimes with other girls but sometimes alone. I wondered if she wished things could be different.

One Saturday in January several weeks after our trip, I learned of a friend's connection to the home in New Orleans where I was born. Carrie was out of town and, after walking the dogs, I met Tommy and Addie Louis at the home in Jackson where he grew up. His father had died a year earlier, they'd sold his house, and I'd offered to help move a few pieces of furniture to their own house around the corner. Tommy was going through old papers when I got there, deciding what to keep and what to throw away. Because they had adopted Lucie, I thought they might be interested in hearing about what I found when I went through the papers at the home where I grew up. When I told them about finding the notes Mama wrote when she got the call from the home in New Orleans and learned that she and Daddy would soon have a son, Addie said she got chills. Addie, who grew up in New Orleans, then asked me the name of the maternity home. When I told her, she asked if it was on Washington Avenue. I said that's the one. Then it was her turn to tell me something. More than 30 years earlier, when the home was for abused children and before she married Tommy, Addie had worked as an unpaid intern in the building where I was born.

In Catholic theology the Annunciation is the visit by the archangel Gabriel to the Virgin Mary in which he announces that she will soon be the mother of a baby boy. The Feast of the Annunciation commemorating Gabriel's visit is celebrated on March 25 each year. Mama wasn't Mary and I'm sure no Jesus, but it pleases me to know that the home from which the social worker called Mama to announce that she would soon be the mother of a baby boy was located on the corner of Washington Avenue and Annunciation Street.

Chapter 52

Reunions like those I read about on the Facebook page for Methodist Home Hospital are of recent origin. During Julie's lifetime it was extraordinarily difficult for birth mothers and the children they surrendered to find each other. The premise was that it was better to keep them apart, for the mother and child who were separated at birth to remain separated forever. Records were maintained in strict confidence and officials fought efforts to release them as they did in my case. But opposition to reuniting birth mothers and their children has faded and websites such as Ancestry and 23andme have made it possible for them to find each other simply by submitting DNA samples. Court proceedings such as those that led to my being found are rarely necessary.

While in the midst of writing this, I learned a story about another successful reunion that also involved Facebook but not Methodist Home Hospital. I was contacted by a woman employed at an insurance agency in the office building where I work. She had learned about me from Eason Leake, who is the chairman of the agency's board of directors, and wanted to meet and hear my story. She said she was adopted as an infant and was searching for her birth mother. She came upstairs one afternoon and we exchanged stories, though I had little advice to offer about how to find her birth mother because I had done nothing to find mine. She knew the hospital where she was born but little else. She said she had submitted a DNA sample to Ancestry.com, but so far she had no leads. I wished her luck.

Months later I got an email from her announcing that she'd

found her mother. She made another trip upstairs to tell me all about it. She reported that her DNA matched that of a woman who was 101 years old and living in a nursing home in the Mississippi Delta. From the test results there was no way to know their exact relationship or even whether the woman was related to her mother or her father, but she decided to find out what she could. She found the elderly woman's daughter-in-law on Facebook and sent her a message. The daughter-in-law soon responded and volunteered to help. She was not aware of anyone in the elderly woman's family who could be one of the adoptee's parents, but she promised to contact everyone in the family and provide them with details, including the adoptee's date of birth.

Not long after she did so, the adoptee got a call one night from a woman in Tennessee. After identifying herself, the woman said she thought she was the adoptee's mother, that she'd had a baby on the same day the adoptee was born. The woman couldn't be sure, however, because she'd been told in the hospital that her baby was a boy. But another DNA test confirmed that the two women were mother and daughter. The hospital staff had lied about the baby's gender, presumably to make any search for her more difficult and help keep it all a secret. The adoptee told me her mother had just come to Jackson to meet her, the reunion was happy, and she'd been welcomed into the family. She had communicated with her two younger half siblings, including her sister in New York, with whom she spoke and corresponded often.

The same week I met with the adoptee, an old friend at work who knew I was writing about my adoption told me he had a story to share with me. He said his sister-in-law from Tennessee had just come to Jackson. The purpose of her trip was to meet the daughter she'd given up for adoption when she was in college more than 40 years earlier. He didn't know the daughter existed until that week. Nor did he know that the daughter and I knew each other. Though a woman who lives in Tennessee is the only connection between my old friend and my new one, the uncle and niece work one floor apart in the same building. Until that week neither one knew about the other.

Genealogy services and DNA testing have not only facilitated reunions of birth mothers and children who were separated long ago, they have also made it possible to find other long-lost relatives and identify long-dead ancestors. A friend at my firm, Barry Cockrell, discovered that he is a direct descendant of a host of famous people, including William the Conqueror, who became the first Norman king of England following his victory at the Battle of Hastings in 1066; King John, who was forced to sign the Magna Carta securing the rights of English citizens in 1215; and William and Mary Randolph, whose other descendants include Thomas Jefferson, Robert E. Lee, a Chief Justice of the United States Supreme Court, the first president of the Continental Congress, and the first Attorney General of the United States. I asked Barry what went wrong along the way, why he's just an obscure lawyer like me. He just shrugged.

Chapter 53

I did nothing to identify or search for my birth father for more than a decade after I learned about Julie and the circumstances of my birth. I got on with my life and rarely thought about it. I had never had a burning desire to know before then, and I obviously still didn't. But in the course of researching and writing this story, I spoke with two people who told me they believed they knew who my father was and they identified the same man. Lewis Bettman had told me he thought he knew when I first spoke to him in the summer of 2004. Fourteen years later he gave me a name. Sid gave me the same name. Both said they thought Julie was dating the young man, who would now be an old man if he was still alive, when she got pregnant in the fall of 1956.

After they told me, I couldn't resist doing some research and I found the man quickly on the internet. He was a retired surgeon. I also found him on Facebook with a current photo and I later saw a college-era photo of him standing beside Julie in a family scrapbook. I was skeptical—I look just like Julie but nothing like him and his name is not Scott—but I decided to try to contact him. Whether he's my father or not, he dated Julie, and I was trying to find out all I could about her. I sent him a message on Facebook saying I was Julie's son. I did not suggest that he was my father but said I knew they went to college together and that I would like to speak to him. He didn't respond so a couple of weeks later I found a street address and wrote him a letter saying the same thing. He didn't respond to that either. Then I checked Facebook again and found he had canceled his account.

His actions were suspicious but hardly conclusive. Maybe his quitting Facebook was a coincidence or perhaps he's not my father and thought I just wanted his money. Or maybe he is my father, but he's an unwed father who still can't be bothered. But whatever the case, it doesn't bother me. Like Julie, he was only 18 when I was born and he almost certainly had no say in what happened to me. And if he is my father, chances are he has a family that he never told about me. I didn't want to cause him any distress by continuing to try to contact him, so I decided to let it go.

But if I meet him someday and he is my father, I will thank him for my life. And I will show him pictures of the grandchildren and great-grandchildren he doesn't know he has, and I will thank him for them. There are eight of us—my three children, four grandchildren, and me—who would not exist were it not for him and the accidental pregnancy in the fall of 1956. And that's just so far. There will no doubt be more to come when one or both of my sons have children, when my grandchildren grow up and have children of their own, and when their children have children too. A cascade of lives, starting with mine and continuing with those who won't be born until long after I'm gone, all resulting from a single unplanned pregnancy. It sounds amazing and unique, but in truth it's neither. How many of us alive in the world today are here only because of an accidental pregnancy somewhere along the way? I would place a healthy wager that it's every single one of us.

So if I meet my father, it will make for yet another revelation. But if I never meet him, that will be alright too. He may be a very good man, but he couldn't be as good as the man who raised me.

Chapter 54

One of the challenges in writing a memoir, at least this memoir, is that the story isn't over and it's hard to know when to stop. I learned many things about this story while writing it and, even after my manuscript was already in the publisher's hands in the summer of 2019, I learned one more thing that I needed to add. So I told the publisher to stop the presses, sat down at my computer, and typed this chapter.

Paul Coggins is exactly two months younger than I am. He was born on September 3, 1957. He and I grew up together in Tupelo, became very close in high school, and were fraternity brothers at Ole Miss. He now lives north of Dallas, where he has a landscape business. We rarely see each other, but we stay in touch.

Paul and I had great times together. Paul would borrow his stepfather's old Ford pickup and we would ride around in the country outside Tupelo drinking beer after school or after we got off from our summer job building swimming pools. We didn't drink too much, but it was still an adventure because there was so much play in the steering wheel that Paul had to turn it halfway around before the steering engaged and the truck started to turn. I never asked to drive.

The truck provided another benefit as well. Paul's family owned a small convenience store just west of downtown called West End Grocery. The store advertised during intermission at the Lee Drive-In theater in south Tupelo, which meant that the truck and everyone in it could get in for free. Paul would round up a group of us with lawn chairs and a cooler, back into a spot, and we would set up in the bed of the pickup. Sometimes we paid attention to the movie, but sometimes we didn't.

Paul and Dan Purnell both excelled on the high school wrestling team. Paul was strong as a bull, weighed nearly 190, and wrestled in the unlimited weight class. Dan was strong too, but he was barely half as big, wrestling at 98 and then 105. Several times Paul and I sat in a sauna with Dan to provide him with moral support as he tried to sweat off a last pound or two to make weight. Because Paul wrestled unlimited, he didn't have to make weight. I was on the tennis team and neither did I.

Paul's mother Millie, whom I've known all my life, is a delightful woman with a dry sense of humor, the kind you have to listen to closely or you might miss something good. Paul and I often tried her patience, but she always forgave us, and I was always welcome in their home. I spent a great deal of time there when we were in high school. I enjoyed Millie's company, and she seemed to take a special interest in me. In the summer of 2019, 44 years after Paul and I graduated from Tupelo High School and left for college, I found out why.

My cousin Phil Ruff is very active in the First Methodist Church in Tupelo. One of the ministries he assists with is serving communion in the homes of elderly church members who are no longer able to attend services. Millie, who was almost 92 by the summer of 2019, was one of the members he took communion to then. On one of Phil's visits Millie told him something about me that she'd never told me. In the summer of 1957, when I was born and she was pregnant with Paul, she was working at the Lee County Health Department in downtown Tupelo where one of her duties was handling the paperwork and coordinating adoptions in Lee County. She disclosed to Phil that she handled mine. She also told Phil that she often thought to herself when I was at their house that she knew things about me that I didn't know. But for more than 60 years, in all the time we spent together, she never breathed a word of it to me.

After Phil told me what Millie told him, I talked to Paul and then called Millie, whose mind and memory were still sharp. The

Welfare Department where she worked and the Health Department where Mama worked were in the same building in the 1950s —the City County building in downtown Tupelo—and the two of them became friends before Paul and I were born. She told me that Mama and Daddy were the finest of people, she thought the world of them, and she said how fortunate I was that they adopted me. She said I was a cute baby. I said I was fat. She said babies are supposed to be fat. She also said she couldn't wait to read my book.

A few days after I talked to Millie, I turned 62. As Carrie and I were preparing for the house concert we hosted that night, Paul sent me a text message, wished me a happy birthday, and forwarded a message Millie had asked him to pass along. In her message she wrote:

> I have tried to look back and think about Brooks's adoption. He was born in July and I went on maternity leave in August. I have forgotten the exact date Margaret and Paul made their request for a baby boy, but I know it was many months before Brooks was born and their request was granted. There was a great deal of paperwork that went back and forth between maternity homes and the Welfare Department. Adoptions are special and affect many lives. They were always taken very seriously.
>
> When Paul and Margaret got the call that the perfect baby for them had been born, they were overjoyed and made the trip to New Orleans to pick him up and bring him home to Tupelo. One day while I was on leave, Margaret dressed Brooks up and brought him down to the City County building to see everyone. She called me so I could come downtown

and see him too. He was the cutest baby and she let everyone hold him, which was great. A perfect match. I have been fortunate to watch Brooks grow up and be a successful adult.

I have always thought that we were more particular than God in placing babies. Tell Brooks this part of his story and that I'm really happy to be a part of it.

We had already settled on the title of the book when I read Millie's message. We decided not to change it, but her message tempted me. More Particular Than God would have been a fine title.

Chapter 55

Carrie and I had an enjoyable weekend in Tulsa when we went to visit Sid in April 2018. He treated us to lunch at Southern Hills Country Club, which has one of the finest golf courses in the country. He gave us a tour of the clubhouse and showed us the photos and scorecards from the major golf championships that have been played there since the club was founded in the midst of the Depression. The prize money for first place when Tommy Bolt won the U.S. Open at Southern Hills in 1958, the year after I was born, was $8,000. When Tiger Woods won the PGA there in 2007, the year my grandson Eason was born, it was $1,260,000, more than 150 times as much. On the day we were at the club, it was very cold for April, too cold for golf, and we had the place to ourselves.

Sid then took us on a driving tour of Tulsa and showed us the two beautiful homes Sidney Davis built, where Betty grew up and the family gathered for holidays. After that he drove us through downtown Tulsa and we saw the Robert W. Davis building named for Brenda's late husband, a successful banker. We then went back to Sid's condo and watched the third round of the Masters. I realized later that Julie died the day after the Masters ended 32 years earlier.

That evening Sid took us to one of his favorite dinner spots. His daughter Margo and her husband Reid joined us. We had a fine time and drank toasts to meeting new family members. Like me, Margo is a litigator at a big law firm. Sid, the proud father, has told me more than once that she was the valedictorian of her law school class. Margo's practice is similar to mine, but her age is not. Though we are first cousins, I was 60 at the time of our trip to Tulsa and she was 29. Before we parted, Margo asked if we could meet the next morning for breakfast and we agreed on a time and a place.

Amy the Dancing Bear, written by singer Carly Simon, is one of my favorite children's books. The book involves a contest of wills between parent and child. Amy's mother wants Amy to go to bed, but Amy wants to stay up and dance even more. She truly loves to dance and begs her mother, "Please, oh please, let me just dance a little more, just a little more."

Amy's mother can "hardly refuse such a pleasant little argument" so she finds other things to do. She washes the dishes and polishes the knives and forks "with a special pink polish until each was so shiny you could see your reflection in it if you felt like it." She makes herself a glass of iced tea and listens to a piano sonata. She falls asleep in a bubble bath. All the while, alone in her room, Amy dances.

It's a beautiful book, beautifully written and illustrated. Over the three decades since it was published, I have read it many times, first to Ann Lowrey, then to Cliff and Paul, then to Ada Brooks, Eason, Collins, and Elsa Gray. I read it to Carrie when we babysat for the grandchildren one night the week we met and again the night I proposed to her. It's out of print now, but I've bought many used copies over the years and given them to friends as baby presents.

I was reminded of Amy and her mother when Carrie and I met Sid, Margo, and Reid for breakfast in Tulsa on Sunday morning. After we had eaten and the dishes were cleared away, Margo presented me with a gift, a sterling silver serving fork that had been passed down to her from Julie. Sandy had inherited it from Julie in the late 1980s and given it to Margo more than 20 years later as a wedding present. It was the only thing of Julie's that Margo owned, but now she was giving it to me. Reid told us that Margo had polished it after they got home from dinner the night before. I pictured her at the kitchen sink, using the same special pink polish Amy's mother used, holding up the serving fork, admiring her work, and seeing her reflection.

When Carrie and I got home from Tulsa, I held the serving fork that had been held by the mother I never knew. I turned it over in my hands. Like the knives and forks Amy's mother had polished, I could see my reflection in it. I wondered if Julie ever looked at the fork and saw her reflection. It was a generous gift from the cousin I had just met.

After studying the fork, I went to our bookshelves and pulled down my only remaining copy of *Amy the Dancing Bear* and read it for the umpteenth time. When I had bought several used copies to give as baby presents years earlier, I opened this one, discovered it was signed by Carly Simon, and decided to keep it. But now I decided to give it away too. The next day I took it to my office, wrapped it up, and mailed it to Margo. While finishing this manuscript a year later, I learned that she and Reid were expecting their first child, a boy. I hope they read *Amy the Dancing Bear* to him.

Chapter 56

Two months after our trip to Tulsa, Carrie and I drove north to Iowa City for me to attend a writing workshop at the University of Iowa. Before the trip I contacted Pearson Buell, Sandy's middle son, and arranged to have lunch along the way with him, his wife Lisa, and Sandy in Lake St. Louis, the suburb west of St. Louis where they live. He suggested that Carrie and I meet with him and Lisa at their home before picking Sandy up for lunch. When I asked what time, he said nine o'clock. Carrie and I wondered what we would do all morning with a couple we had never met, but we found out when we got there. Pearson and Lisa could not have been nicer. Pearson told us stories about Julie and Sandy, and Lisa showed us scrapbooks filled with old photos, including pictures of Sandy's wedding to Joe Buell in which Julie was the maid of honor and of Julie's wedding to Lee Farnham several years later when they swapped roles.

Pearson said he and his brothers loved it when Julie came to visit and when she went on trips with them. She was a sister to Sandy but to them she was like a movie star. She was nothing like their other relatives. Aunts and uncles were supposed to be old and boring. Julie was neither. She was the cool aunt—beautiful, glamorous, charismatic—and dressed like she'd just come from a photo shoot for a fashion magazine. When she was there with her big smile and laugh, she was the life of the party. People were drawn to her. Sandy was aware of Julie's troubles, but Julie hid them from the boys. She sure seemed happy to them. Perhaps she paused and took a deep breath before she knocked on the door.

Without fail Julie arrived bearing gifts, each one carefully selected for the intended recipient. They invariably were things the Buells never would have bought for themselves. She presented Pearson with a pair of patchwork quilt jeans she had brought home from France, which made him feel cooler than he'd ever felt. When he and Lisa got engaged, the first gift they received was from Julie.

And Pearson and Lisa returned the kindness to Carrie and me, loading our car with things that had belonged to Julie, including cookbooks filled with her notes, a children's book, novels, dishes, and serving plates. Best of all, they gave us a portrait of Julie painted when she was in her early teens. She was already a beauty.

Ann Lowrey was born just before nine o'clock on Sunday night, May 13, 1984. It was Mother's Day. Her birthday is exactly five weeks before Ada Brooks's. When May 13 again falls on Sunday, Ann Lowrey's birthday is on Mother's Day and Ada's is on Father's Day. It happened again in 2018, though Carrie and I could not celebrate with Ada on her birthday because we were in Lake St. Louis having lunch with Sandy, Pearson, and Lisa.

To make up for being gone, we hosted a belated birthday party for Ada Brooks at Camp Carrie when we got home. Before the guests arrived, we showed Ann Lowrey and Ada the portrait of the grandmother and great-grandmother they never knew. When I asked how old they thought Julie was when it was painted, Carrie pointed out that there was a date, 1952, by the artist's signature. When I saw the date, something dawned on me. The portrait was painted the year Julie turned 14 and Pearson and Lisa gave it to us the day Ada Brooks turned 14. I took two photos, one of the portrait and one of Ada—my birth mother and granddaughter, the same age, both beautiful.

A week after we hosted Ada's birthday party, we hosted a house concert on my birthday. Before our guests arrived, I searched for the best place to hang Julie's portrait. I picked a spot in our hallway next to two of Mama's drawings and summoned Carrie to make sure she approved. She said it was perfect and started to head back to the kitchen, but then she stopped herself. By the summer of 2018 Julie had been gone 32 years, Mama almost 19. Carrie did not know either of them and they never met each other. Carrie stared at the three pieces of art and then smiled and pointed out something that had not dawned on me. She said neither of my mothers could have imagined that Julie's portrait and Mama's drawings would one day hang beside each other on the same wall.

And it was true. Julie surrendered me for adoption eight days after I was born and never saw me again. She didn't know my name, where I lived, or what became of me. And yet, 61 years to the day after she gave birth to me, I hung her portrait in my home next to drawings by the mother who adopted and raised me. Julie never could have imagined it.

Ten weeks after I was born, Mama got the call from New Orleans and learned that she would finally get the baby boy she and Daddy wanted. And now, more than six decades later, hanging next to her drawings was a portrait of the girl she learned about that day, the girl from a western state who liked sports, dancing, and cooking and whose identity was a secret. Mama never could have imagined it. Until the summer of 2018 I never could have imagined it either.

Months after Pearson and Lisa gave us the portrait of Julie, they gave us another one. When I returned home on the day I learned that Addie Louis had worked as an intern in the building where I was born, there was a package leaning against our front door. The return address was for the Buells in Lake St. Louis. Because Carrie was out of town, I waited to open it until she got home. Inside was a framed photograph of Julie in her wedding dress. Both she and the dress were beautiful. The photo was taken when she married Lee Farnham in Tulsa in April 1964. The reception following the ceremony was held at Southern Hills Country Club, where Sid took Carrie and me to lunch, also in April but 54 years later.

When Julie and Lee got married in Tulsa, I was 500 miles away in Tupelo, just about to finish the first grade. Only a handful of the hundreds of guests who attended the wedding and reception knew that Julie had given birth to a baby boy nearly seven years earlier. Sandy knew, Betty and Herb Smith almost certainly knew, and Sidney and Louise Davis may have. But Sid Smith, who was about to turn 15, did not. Nor did Brenda Boone, Julie's friend and roommate. Julie had even concealed it from the man she was marrying. She didn't tell Lee until years later when they were living in Colombia. I wonder if she thought about me during the ceremony or reception, if she worried what would happen if Lee learned her secret. Julie's wedding was different from one that took place on the same weekend in April but 42 years later. When Ann Lowrey and Paul got married in 2006, the bride's beautiful child, who was not a secret, was the flower girl.

So now Carrie and I have two portraits of Julie in our home. When I look at them, I stop and think, but for her, there would be no me.

Chapter 57

There are striking similarities in the two stories that unfolded nearly half a century apart—the story about Julie and me in 1957 and the one about Ann Lowrey and Ada Brooks in 2004. Julie got pregnant when she was a freshman in college, Ann Lowrey when she was a sophomore, both during the fall. My birthday and Ada Brooks's are only 16 days apart. We have both been blessed with wonderful parents, Mama and Daddy for me, Ann Lowrey and Paul the Groom for her. But our biological fathers did not marry our mothers or support them and did nothing to help raise us. Ada Brooks doesn't know her birth father and I don't know mine. But that doesn't change the fact that we would not exist without them. They, along with Julie and Ann Lowrey, gave us life. In fact, Ada Brooks owes her life to two unwed fathers—mine and hers. Without both of them there would be no Grand Prize.

In the weeks after learning about Julie and the search to find me, including the litigation in Oklahoma and Louisiana, I told the story many times to friends and family. Some asked how it made me feel, what it was like to learn of my origin and see photos of the woman who gave birth to me. In truth, writing about the two parents who raised me has been more emotional than learning about the one who didn't. I always knew I was adopted, it never troubled me, and learning the story did not have a profound impact on me. So when friends asked how learning the story affected me, I said I wasn't sure. But I was sure of one thing: It was a good story. I would have thought it was a good story even if it was about someone else. And the most amazing thing about it was the timing—what was

happening in the present at exactly the same time I was learning about the past.

The day Daddy called to tell me about the message from the lawyer in New Orleans was June 8, 2004. I called the lawyer that day and first talked to Ben Faulkner the next day. I spoke to Lewis Bettman, Sid Smith, and Edith Morris and received the photos of Julie and her parents and cousins over the course of the next several weeks. While all of this was happening, in the midst of learning about Julie and her family, I became a grandfather. My adoption file, from which I learned that I began life as Scott Francis, was mailed to me from New Orleans on June 17, the same day we took Ann Lowrey to the hospital and Ada Brooks was born.

Ann Lowrey was as curious about Julie and the story as I was. Both before and after Ada was born, she called me at work every day to find out the latest. When I got the adoption file, she read it from cover to cover. She was delighted that the social worker had described me as a husky child who jabbered constantly. I reminded her that she wasn't exactly skinny or quiet when she was a baby either. A week after we brought Ada Brooks home from the hospital, the photos of Julie, Betty, and Tom Francis, Ada's great-grandmother and great-great-grandparents, were delivered to my office. I came home early that afternoon to show them to Ann Lowrey. She was waiting in the den, Ada asleep in her lap.

I pulled the photos from the envelope one at a time for her to study. She took her time and held them up so she could see me and them at the same time and compare features. When I showed her the last one, the one that looked like a much younger me with a wig, she smiled and shook her head. Ann Lowrey looks very much like me so she looks very much like Julie. Ada Brooks looks like Julie too.

And I wish they all could have known each other. I know they would have enjoyed each other's company. Julie would have been the cool grandmother just as she was the cool aunt. But unless she had changed her ways, she would not have been the cool grandmother for long. Julie was only 45 when Ann Lowrey was born, but she died a month before Ann Lowrey's second birthday. On our trip to Tulsa Sid told us he thought Julie just gave up, that she quit caring. Given the ultimatum—quit drinking or die—she still didn't quit. But maybe having a beautiful, precocious granddaughter would have given Julie something to care about. Maybe it would have given her the strength to quit. And if she had quit, she could have gone on to become the cool great-grandmother. She would have been only 65 when Ada Brooks was born.

After Ann Lowrey looked at all the photos, she looked down at Ada Brooks, who was just over a week old, the same age I was when Julie signed the papers and saw me for the last time. Without looking up, Ann Lowrey then said the one thing that makes her story different from Julie's and Ada's story different from mine, the one thing that has allowed me to see Ada grow into a beautiful, accomplished young lady. She said she was grateful to live in a time when she could keep her baby.

I am grateful for that too, extraordinarily grateful. And though I wonder what might have been, I am also grateful that Julie lived in a time when she could not keep hers. I had wonderful parents who gave me a wonderful life. I would not trade being their son for all the tea in China. But I do have one regret. For Julie's sake I wish she could have known of the grace that came with the giving away. When she signed the papers and saw me for the last time, I wish she could have known that she gave me the whole world that day.

Acknowledgements

I have many people to thank for their contributions to this story. My friends Michael de Leeuw of New Jersey and Lorraine Mann of the Scottish Highlands, both excellent writers, gave freely of their time and talents in reading the manuscript and making helpful suggestions. Michael has now lent his valuable assistance to me on both of my books. He also provided me with an important fact for this one. I knew my birthplace was on Washington Avenue, but it was Michael who told me it was on the corner of Washington Avenue and Annunciation Street.

I greatly appreciate the kindness and generosity of Julie's friends and family—my second family—and their willingness to spend time sharing with me what they know about the mother I never knew. Sid Smith, Sandy Buell, Lee Farnham, Lewis Bettman, and Brenda Boone were all generous with their time. Pearson and Lisa Buell not only shared their memories of Julie with Carrie and me, but they gave me two portraits of Julie that now hang in our home. I am also grateful to three of my cousins who are related to me but not to each other. Elizabeth Keckler recorded her interview with Daddy, Margo Shipley presented me with Julie's serving fork, and Lee Cheney shared with me the amazing story about the downfall and redemption of our grandfather.

And I am thankful to Doc Schneider for writing a song about my story and letting me use the title of his song in the title of my book. I give special thanks to Carrie, the World's Best Wife, for encouraging me to pursue and complete this project and giving me helpful advice along the way. And finally, I thank Julie for having me, Mama and Daddy for raising me, and Ann Lowrey for giving me Ada Brooks and Ada's little brothers and sister.

Also available from

WordCrafts Press

Geezer Stories: The Care & Feeding of Old People
by Laura Mansfield

An Introspective Journey: A Memoir of Living with Alzheimer's
by Paula Sarver

Against Every Hope: India, Mother Teresa, and a Baby Girl
by Bonnie Tinsley

A Scarlet Cord of Hope
by Sheryl Griffin

Confounding the Wise: A Celebration of Life, Love, Laugher & Adoption
by Dan Kulp

Pressing Forward
by April Poytner

Curtain Call
by Lyneta Smith

www.WordCrafts.net